FRETBOARD THEORY, TECHNIQUE, AND COMPREHENSION FOR

THE

DEVELOPING

GUITARIST

VMG

VANDERZYDE MEDIA GROUP, LLC

P.O. Box 310105 New Braunfels, TX 78131

ISBN 979-8-9865420-0-3

LCCN: 2022912550

Visit thomasvanderzyde.com for contact and additional information.

Pre Material

Post Material

I

FRETBOARD THEORY

II

APPLIED PHYSICAL TECHNIQUE

III

APPLIED TEMPORAL TECHNIQUE

TUNING, DIAGRAMS, AND TABS

For best results, an electronic or vibration-based tuner is highly recommended. That being said, every guitarist should be able to tune their guitar by ear. If not in perfect concert pitch, then at least in tune with itself. This can be achieved through harmonics and/or relative frets, like so:

Diagrams are to be read as theoretical fretboard information with no commitments to time or note order. They are designed to be a visual reference for patterns or collections of notes, and provide a guiding framework when exploring the fretboard. Every diagram in this book will be represented with vertical frets and horizontal strings.

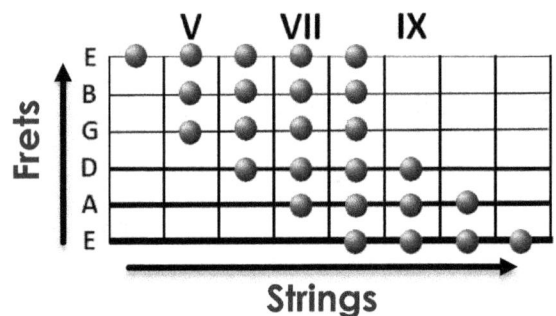

Tablature is a fantastic resource for seeing *where* to play, but not necessarily the best for *when*. Be sure to reference the rhythms in the sheet music above each line of tab to know when and how fast to play:

TO THE STUDENT

First, *thank you* for picking up a copy of my work. I sincerely hope it serves you well on your journey to musical development. The world of guitar is getting bigger by the day, so I've done my best to curate a selection of material that will give you the tools necessary to find your way through such a labyrinth.

Special care has been taken not to tell you *what* to play, but rather how certain sounds and colors are achieved through guided analysis. It is the goal of this material not to give you immediate answers, but to supply you with information to use when forming your own original thoughts and drawing your own conclusions. The end result should be an exploration of the experience a guitar offers, not just a direct regurgitation of an exercise or passage. Really take the time to familiarize yourself with the techniques and theory offered, and remember to ask yourself *why* things work the way they work when analyzing various fretboard relationships. This book will give you the toolbox and materials, but at the end of the day nobody will build that house for you. The journey is yours alone, but rest assured I (and google, probably) am here for moral support!

Above all, remember to have fun and find joy in the process. See you on the other side...

THE CEREBRAL

FRETBOARD THEORY

I

THE CHROMATIC LAYOUT

To the untrained eye, the fretboard can be a sea of notes that is rather difficult to navigate through. Rather than seemingly random notes, the developed guitarist sees a road map of possibilities. Each area of the fretboard serves as a tool of expression; a slightly different hue of color. As you play through these notes, do your best to think about not only the name of each pitch, but also the tone and feeling each one offers. Frets one through twelve contain all twelve chromatic pitches, enabling the pattern to start over from fret thirteen to the end of the fretboard (fret 21 or 22 on most guitars).

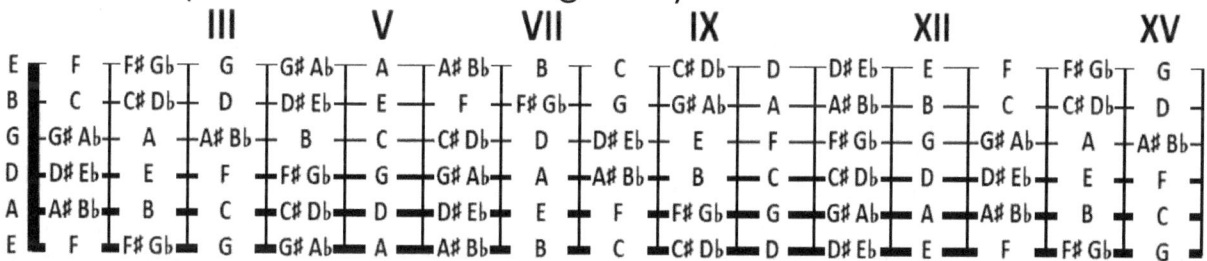

Digesting the vast amount of information that the fretboard offers is no small feat. Just like moving to a new city, you will need time and tools to navigate and understand where you are and where you are going. Think of the diagram below as a road map; a set of road markers to guide you across the city. Memorizing this road map will accelerate your travel time exponentially in the future. This diagram links every E on the fretboard to each other, allowing the player to find every E once they have found one. Notice that the pattern repeats itself every twelve frets, or until there are no more frets to play:

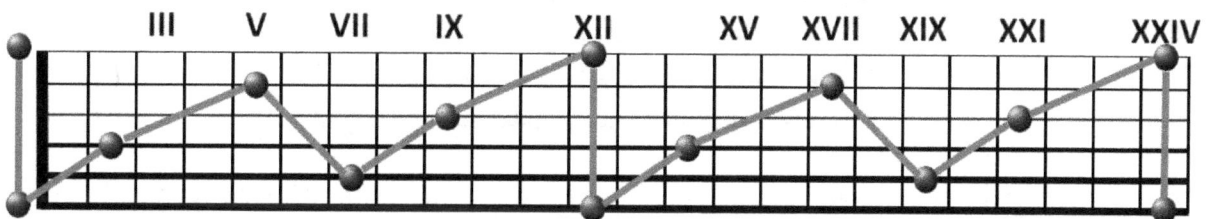

Because the relationship between notes stays the same as fret numbers increase, the entire diagram can be moved up by one fret to find every F, up two frets to find every F#/Gb, up three frets to find every G, and so on.

The guitar's fretboard is an elaborate and unique system. Unlike most instruments, the same note in the same **_octave_*** can be found on the instrument up to six times! Use the diagram below as a reference for fret-relativity across the strings. Notice the change in color and timbre across the fretboard as you play these tones. Notes on the lower frets and thinner strings sound brighter and sharper, while notes on the higher frets and thicker strings sound darker and more mellow.

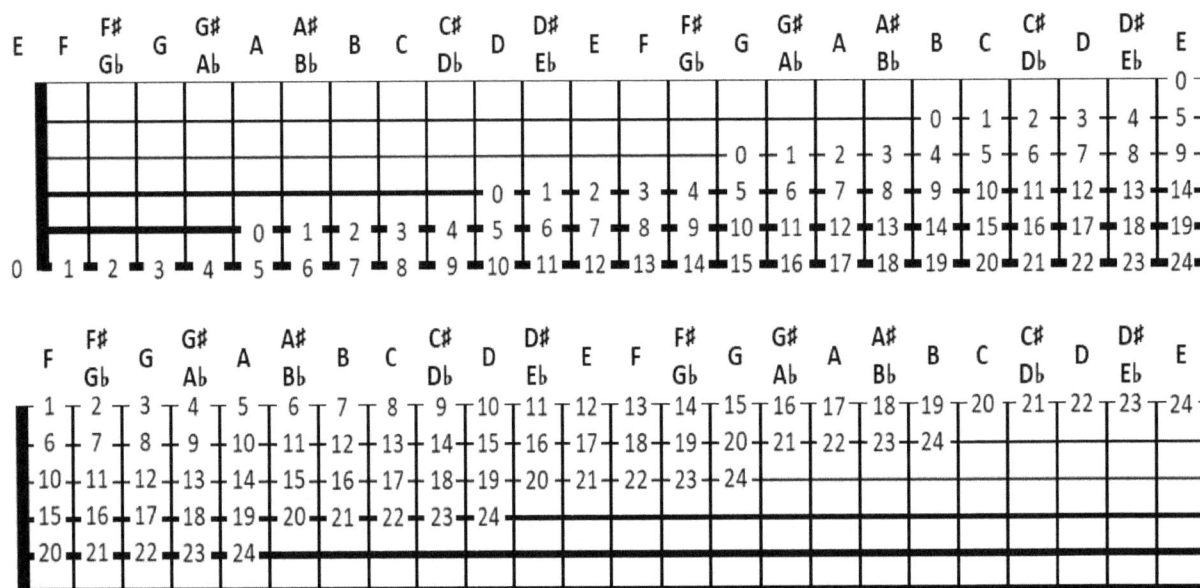

E	F	F#/Gb	G	G#/Ab	A	A#/Bb	B	C	C#/Db	D	D#/Eb	E	F	F#/Gb	G	G#/Ab	A	A#/Bb	B	C	C#/Db	D	D#/Eb	E

```
                                                        0  1  2  3  4  5   (E)
                                      0  1  2  3  4  5  6  7  8  9 10 ...14 (B)
                     0  1  2  3  4  5  6  7  8  9 10 11 12 ...          ..19 (G)
         0  1  2  3  4  5  6  7  8  9 10 11 12 ...                      ..24 (D)
0  1  2  3  4  5  6  7  8  9 10 11 12 13 14 15 16 17 18 19 20 21 22 23 24   (A)
```

F	F#/Gb	G	G#/Ab	A	A#/Bb	B	C	C#/Db	D	D#/Eb	E	F	F#/Gb	G	G#/Ab	A	A#/Bb	B	C	C#/Db	D	D#/Eb	E

```
1  2  3  4  5  6  7  8  9 10 11 12 13 14 15 16 17 18 19 20 21 22 23 24
6  7  8  9 10 11 12 13 14 15 16 17 18 19 20 21 22 23 24
10 11 12 13 14 15 16 17 18 19 20 21 22 23 24
15 16 17 18 19 20 21 22 23 24
20 21 22 23 24
```

Below is an example of a chromatic scale starting on C (open circles), which uses every available pitch within its range. More on this later.

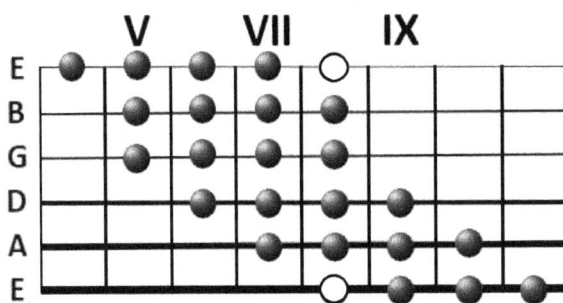

*An **_octave_** is a collection of all twelve chromatic pitches, such as C to C on a piano, or frets one through twelve on a guitar. Pianos have a range of about seven octaves, while guitars have a range of about four.

One common practice among guitarists is the understanding of "**positions**", where the fretboard is chopped up into four-fret sections, with one fret for each left hand (playing hand) finger. For example, fifth position would tell the guitarist that their first finger (pointer) should be placed on fret five, second (middle) on fret six, third (ring) on fret seven, and fourth (pinky) on fret eight, like so:

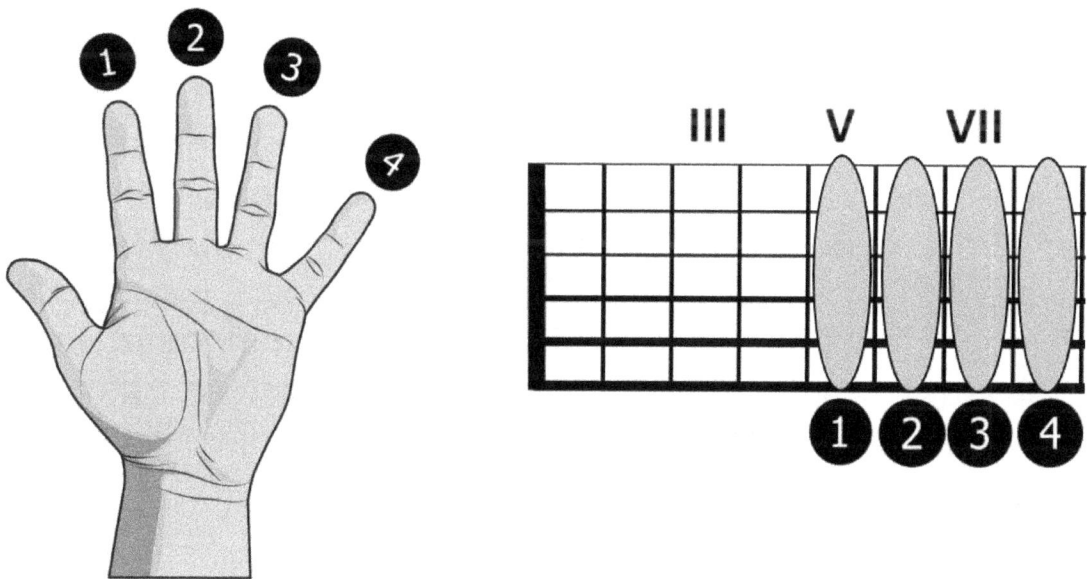

Within any given position anywhere on the fretboard lies at least one of every single pitch (not necessarily in the same octave) somewhere on one of the six strings. Of course, certain positions are more advantageous than others for certain notes, but in theory it is possible to play any series of notes in any given position. This is the concept that seems most inconceivable to developing guitarists and is an understanding that is achieved through hours upon hours of practice. Do not be discouraged when working on fretboard theory, you are not alone! Knowing which position to use and when to use it is a skill that comes with time.

INTERVALS

Interval recognition is a fundamental skill for developing musicians, as it is essentially "spelling" in the musical language. Intervals are used in everything from single vocal lines to the densest symphonic scores. They are a constant measuring stick that is used as a foundation of relativity between notes and instruments.

Put simply, an **interval** is the distance between two pitches, usually measured in half-steps. A **half-step** is the distance between two adjacent notes, like C to C# on a keyboard, or fret one to fret two on any string on a guitar. Pending a few exceptions, seconds, thirds, sixths, and sevenths are generally either major(M), or minor($\overline{m}$) intervals, whereas fourths and fifths are generally referred to as perfect(P) intervals. Intervals that go beyond the octave (ninths through fourteenths) are referred to as **compound intervals**. To convert a "simple" interval into a compound interval, simply keep the interval's description and add seven. For example, a minor third($\overline{m}$3) would compound into a minor tenth($\overline{m}$10).

As stated above, there are some exceptions to naming these intervals. All intervals can be shrunk down (diminished) or stretched out (augmented) by one half step. Minor and perfect intervals can be shrunk to diminished intervals. Major and perfect intervals can be stretched out to augmented intervals. One cannot augment a minor interval as it would become major, just as they could not diminish a major interval as it would become minor. There is no such thing as a diminished second or augmented seventh, as they would be a unison or octave, respectively.

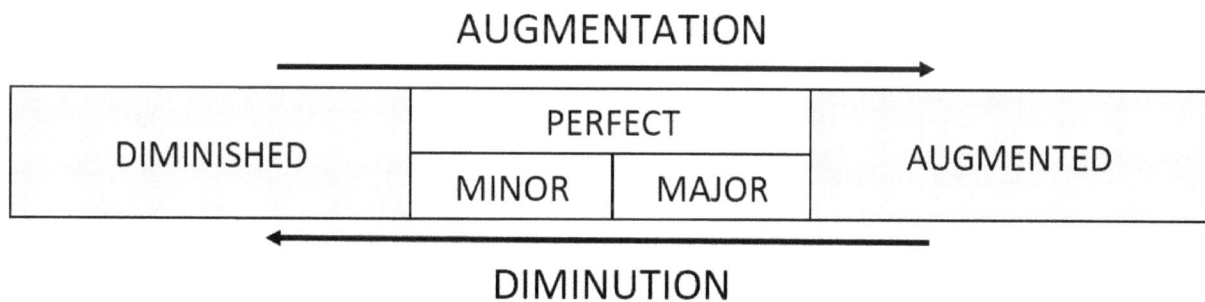

AUGMENTATION

DIMINISHED	PERFECT		AUGMENTED
	MINOR	MAJOR	

DIMINUTION

Just as it is important to know each note within a given position, it is equally important to understand the relationships (or intervals) between them. The following diagram demonstrates these connections. You can think of these relationships as a theoretical endless loop, a pattern that repeats itself every twelve frets in perpetuity. Once a starting note is chosen, the pattern automatically lays out across the fretboard until there are no more frets to play. Notice that there are no fret markers, as this would indicate a permanent, fixed system. The diagram below is a generic, moveable system that only becomes "situated" once the starting note is specified. The intervals are in relation to the starting note, represented by the open circles. Go ahead, pick a note on the fretboard to start on!

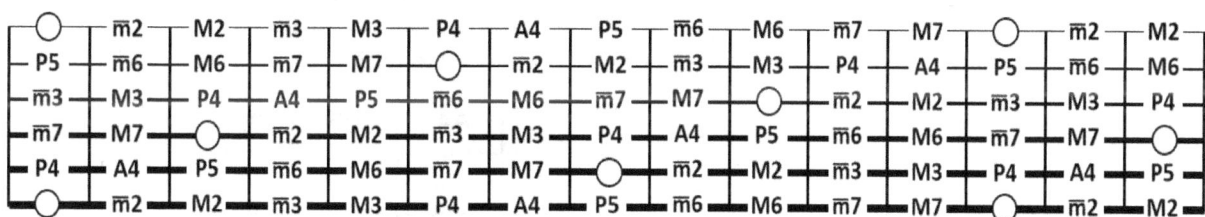

○	m̄2	M2	m̄3	M3	P4	A4	P5	m̄6	M6	m̄7	M7	○	m̄2	M2
P5	m̄6	M6	m̄7	M7	○	m̄2	M2	m̄3	M3	P4	A4	P5	m̄6	M6
m̄3	M3	P4	A4	P5	m̄6	M6	m̄7	M7	○	m̄2	M2	m̄3	M3	P4
m̄7	M7	○	m̄2	M2	m̄3	M3	P4	A4	P5	m̄6	M6	m̄7	M7	○
P4	A4	P5	m̄6	M6	m̄7	M7	○	m̄2	M2	m̄3	M3	P4	A4	P5
○	m̄2	M2	m̄3	M3	P4	A4	P5	m̄6	M6	m̄7	M7	○	m̄2	M2

To further enhance your applied theory in practice, you can break down the information above into individual positions. Memorizing smaller regions at a time will help speed up the learning process and will be much easier to apply to specific melodies or harmonies. These next diagrams break down the intervallic relationships into positions for individual analysis.

○	m̄2	M2	m̄3	M3	P4	A4	P5	m̄6	M6	m̄7	M7	○	m̄2	M2
P5	m̄6	M6	m̄7	M7	○	m̄2	M2	m̄3	M3	P4	A4	P5	m̄6	M6
m̄3	M3	P4	A4	P5	m̄6	M6	m̄7	M7	○	m̄2	M2	m̄3	M3	P4
m̄7	M7	○	m̄2	M2	m̄3	M3	P4	A4	P5	m̄6	M6	m̄7	M7	○
P4	A4	P5	m̄6	M6	m̄7	M7	○	m̄2	M2	m̄3	M3	P4	A4	P5
○	m̄2	M2	m̄3	M3	P4	A4	P5	m̄6	M6	m̄7	M7	○	m̄2	M2

○	m̄2	M2	m̄3
P5	m̄6	M6	m̄7
m̄3	M3	P4	A4
m̄7	M7	○	m̄2
P4	A4	P5	m̄6
○	m̄2	M2	m̄3

m̄2	M2	m̄3	M3
m̄6	M6	m̄7	M7
M3	P4	A4	P5
M7	○	m̄2	M2
A4	P5	m̄6	M6
m̄2	M2	m̄3	M3

M2	m̄3	M3	P4
M6	m̄7	M7	○
P4	A4	P5	m̄6
○	m̄2	M2	m̄3
P5	m̄6	M6	m̄7
M2	m̄3	M3	P4

m̄3	M3	P4	A4
m̄7	M7	○	m̄2
A4	P5	m̄6	M6
m̄2	M2	m̄3	M3
m̄6	M6	m̄7	M7
m̄3	M3	P4	A4

M3	P4	A4	P5
M7	○	m̄2	M2
P5	m̄6	M6	m̄7
M2	m̄3	M3	P4
M6	m̄7	M7	○
M3	P4	A4	P5

P4	A4	P5	m̄6
○	m̄2	M2	m̄3
m̄6	M6	m̄7	M7
m̄3	M3	P4	A4
m̄7	M7	○	m̄2
P4	A4	P5	m̄6

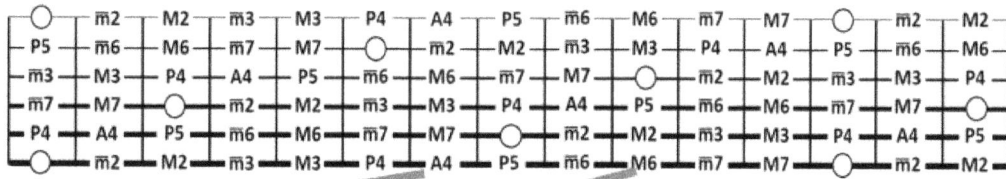

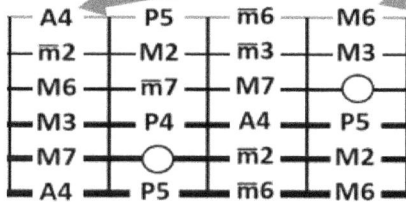

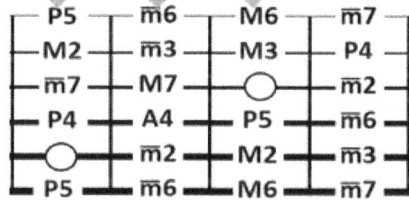

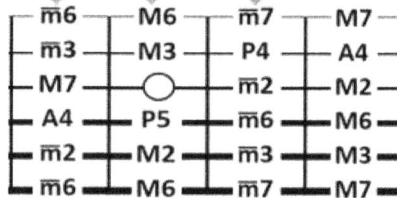

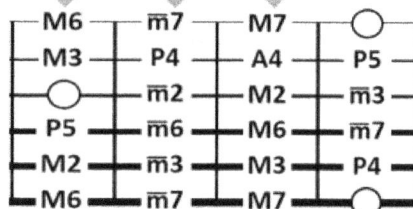

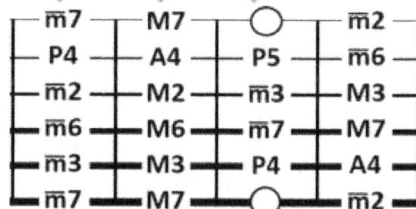

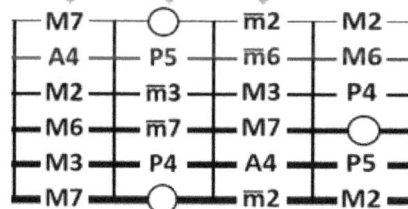

SCALES

Just as the painter has a range of colors on their palette board, the guitarist should have a variety of **scales** at their disposal to add color to their sound. It is important to remember that it's not just about using the scale, but also how the scale is used. Dumping a bucket of paint on a canvas adds color, but using brushstrokes in just the right places adds *dimension*.

Scales come in all shapes and shades; some sound quite vanilla while others have a rather exotic complexion. Scales can have as few as five or as many as twelve notes (within the confines of Western music) and are usually identified with scale degrees. **Scale degrees** correspond to their relative position from the starting note (tonic) and can be raised or lowered with sharps or flats, respectively. Unless otherwise specified, scale degrees default to the standard spacing of the Major Scale as seen below.

Each one of the scales below can be reproduced across various positions on the fretboard. The goal here is not to focus on where the notes are played, but rather the color and emotion each scale offers. As you go through these next examples, think about the feeling each scale brings out, and try to describe it in your own words. Each scale in these examples starts on the note E, so they can be more easily compared to one another.

The **Chromatic Scale** is a kaleidoscope of every color. It includes all 12 chromatic pitches and is the basis from which all other scales are derived.

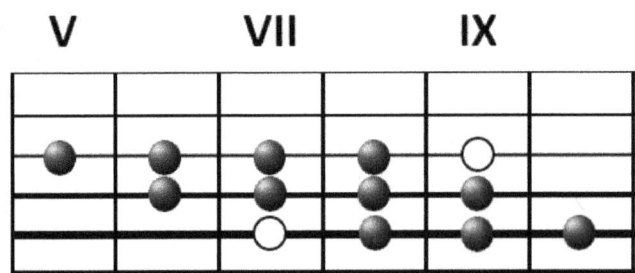

The **Major Scale** is the foundation of Western music and can be found in practically every genre. It is generally characterized as being "happy" and "bright".

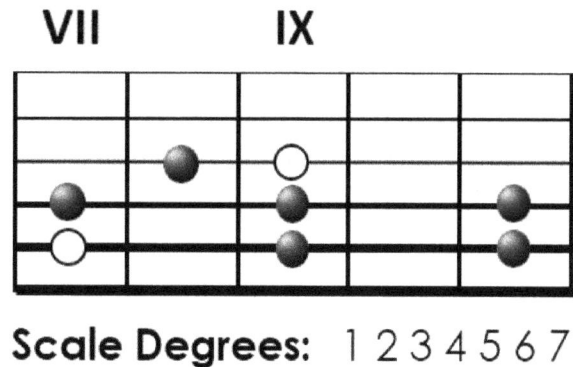

VII   IX

Scale Degrees: 1 2 3 4 5 6 7

The **Natural Minor Scale** is the counter-balance to the Major Scale, as it indicates "sadness" or "darkness".

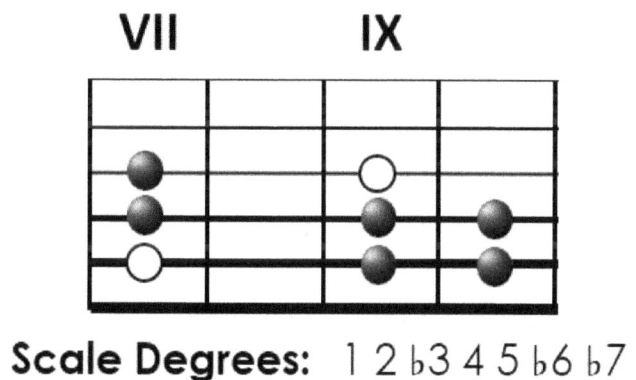

VII   IX

Scale Degrees: 1 2 b3 4 5 b6 b7

The **Harmonic Minor Scale** has a similar characterization to the Natural Minor, with a slight variation in the seventh scale degree. This raised note creates a stronger pull to the scale's starting note, increasing the feeling of tension.

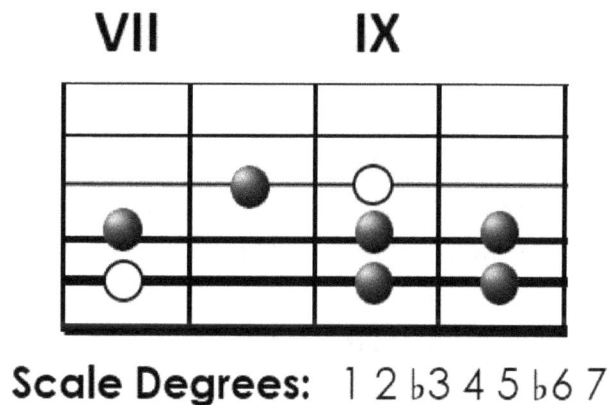

VII   IX

Scale Degrees: 1 2 b3 4 5 b6 7

The **Major Pentatonic Scale** is a universally recognized collection of five notes, and can be found in everything from traditional Japanese music to modern American blues and pop.

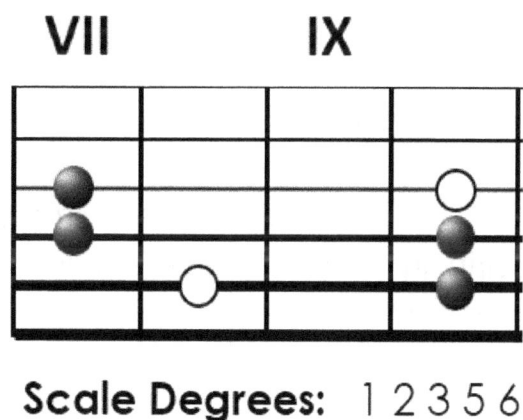

VII   IX

Scale Degrees: 1 2 3 5 6

The **Minor Pentatonic Scale** is the counter-balance to the Major Pentatonic, and has a slightly darker tonality that is great for rock and progressive music.

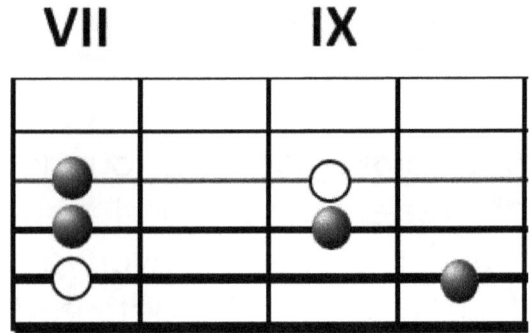

VII　　　**IX**

Scale Degrees:　1 ♭3 4 5 ♭7

The **Neapolitan Minor Scale** imparts a similar color as the Harmonic Minor Scale, with a slightly more dissonant lower register. The second scale degree can be quite powerful when used appropriately.

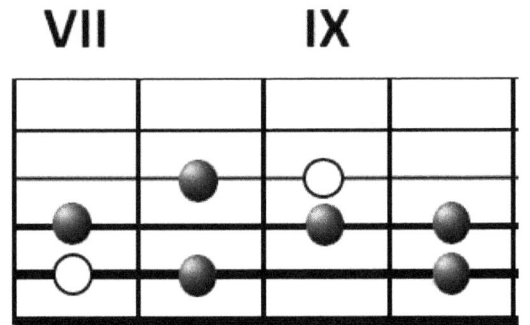

VII　　　**IX**

Scale Degrees:　1 ♭2 ♭3 4 5 ♭6 7

The **Hungarian Minor Scale** provides a little more spice. The right note at the right time can add a very exotic sound to the player's palette.

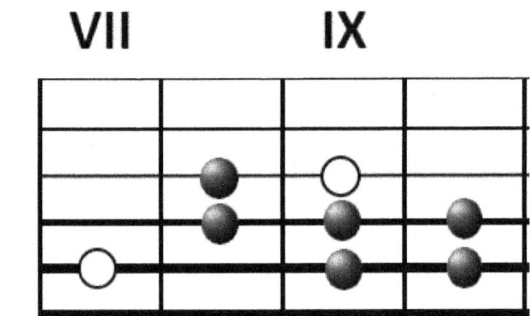

VII　　　**IX**

Scale Degrees:　1 2 ♭3 ♯4 5 ♭6 7

The **Whole Tone Scale** has a very recognizable "floating" feeling about it. This scale is used rather sparingly, as it has little sense of direction.

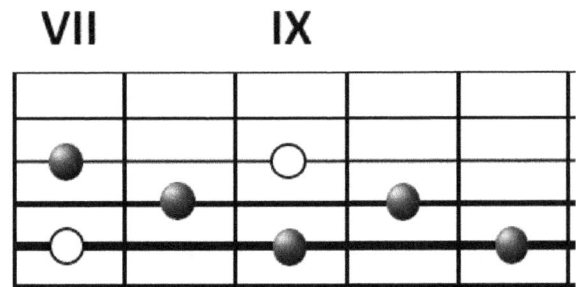

VII　　　**IX**

Scale Degrees:　1 2 3 ♯4 ♯5 ♯6

CHORD QUALITIES AND VOICINGS

Just like scales, chords possess the ability to add color and direction to your sound. There are hundreds upon hundreds of chords (and therefore chord encyclopedias) out there, some go beyond the scope of this book. Learning to play these chords and their variations will come with time, for now the task at hand is to listen and actively internalize the *quality* (unique sound) of each type of chord.

A basic chord consists of three notes: the root, the third, and the fifth. Because **chords** are simply three notes put together, chord quality can be measured with intervals. These combinations of intervals are what determine the unique "recipe" for each chord, and are used to categorize chords into different groups. Below are examples of the most common chord qualities used in music. Again, try not to focus on playing the chord, but instead listening to the chord *quality*. In practice, these formulas can start on any note. For comparison's sake, each chord's root note will start on E in the examples below.

Diminished Formula

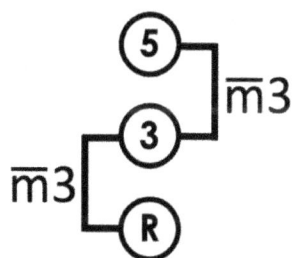

E Diminished Chord

Fifth: B♭

Third: G

Root: E

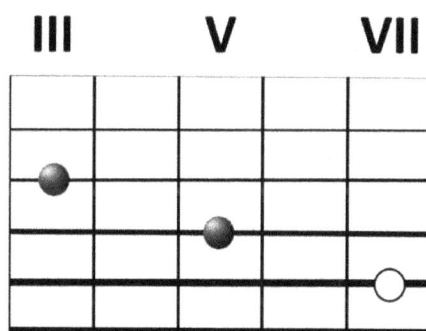

Minor Formula

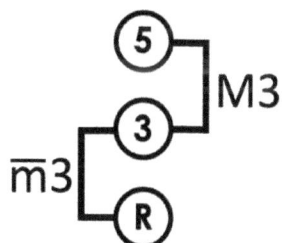

E Minor Chord

Fifth: B

Third: G

Root: E

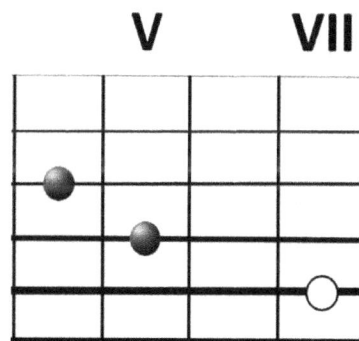

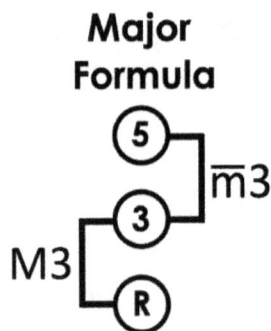

Major Formula

5 ─┐
    ├─ m̄3
3 ─┘
M3 ┐
    └─ R

E Major Chord

Fifth: B

Third: G♯

Root: E

V   VII

Augmented Formula

5 ─┐
    ├─ M3
3 ─┘
M3 ┐
    └─ R

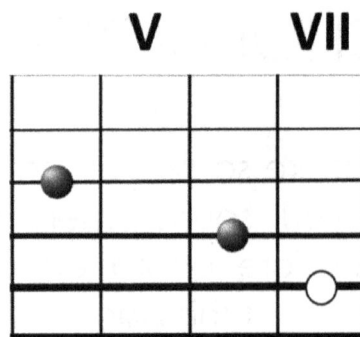

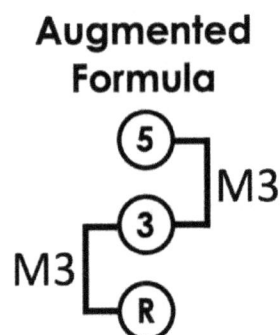

E Augmented Chord

Fifth: B♯

Third: G♯

Root: E

V   VII

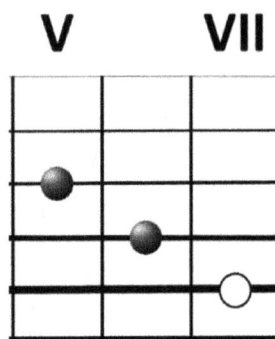

Pitches that have the same sound but different spelling are referred to as **enharmonic**. While the difference between B♭ and A♯ seems irrelevant, it makes a massive difference when it comes to chord function. For example, an E diminished chord is spelled E-G-B♭ (root-third-fifth). It would be incorrect to spell the same chord as E-G-A♯, as that would imply a root-third-fourth relationship. Spelling is vital in music just as it is in English. If your name is Tony and you have to go around constantly spelling your name "Ptoughneigh", you're gonna have a bad time.

The minimum requirement for a chord is three notes, which gives us four combinations or "formulas" (diminished, minor, major, and augmented). The introduction of a fourth note (the seventh) creates additional new colors and unique sounds. Chords with four notes in them are referred to as **seventh chords**, and add depth or complexity to the guitarist's vocabulary. There are six commonly used seventh chords, once again each example's root will start on E:

Fully Diminished 7 Formula

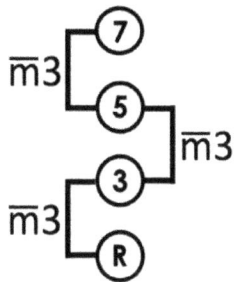

E Fully Diminished 7 Chord

Seventh: D♭

Fifth: B♭

Third: G

Root: E

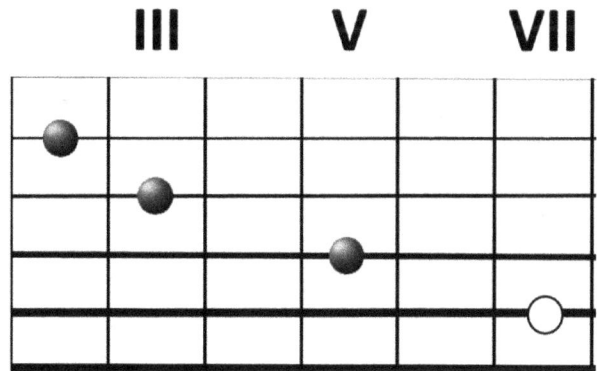

Half Diminished 7 Formula

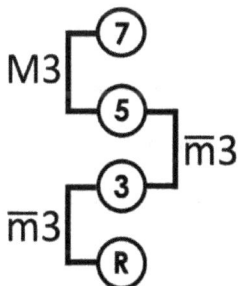

E Half Diminished 7 Chord

Seventh: D

Fifth: B♭

Third: G

Root: E

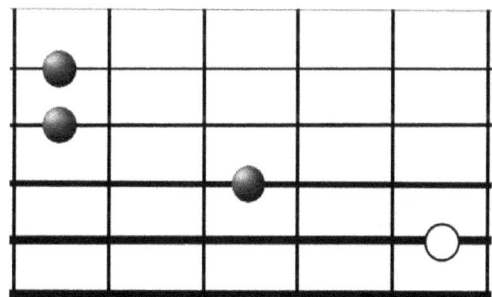

Minor 7 Formula

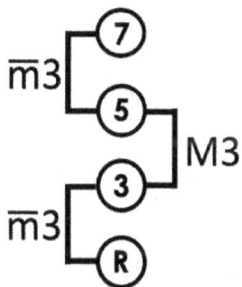

E Minor 7 Chord

Seventh: D

Fifth: B

Third: G

Root: E

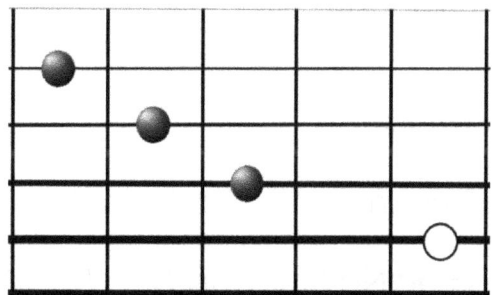

Dominant 7 Formula

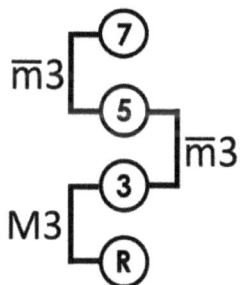

E Dominant 7 Chord

Seventh: D

Fifth: B

Third: G♯

Root: E

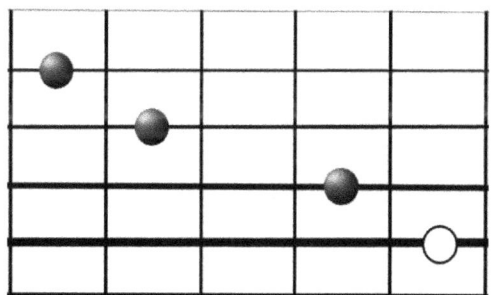

Major 7 Formula

M3, 5, 7, m3, 3, M3, R

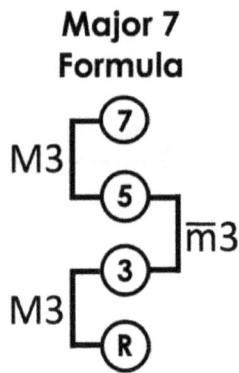

E Major 7 Chord

Seventh: D♯

Fifth: B

Third: G♯

Root: E

V   VII

Augmented 7 Formula

m3, 7, 5, M3, 3, M3, R

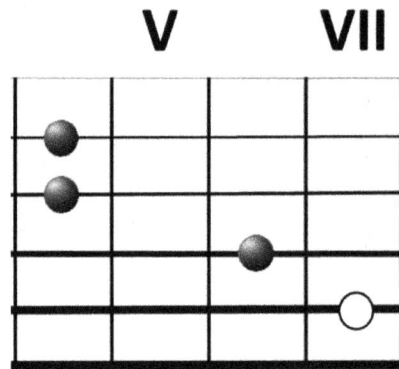

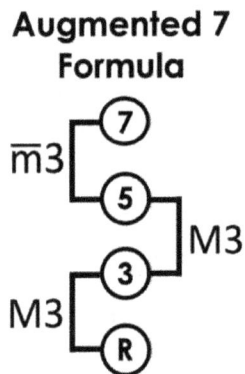

E Augmented 7 Chord

Seventh: D♯

Fifth: B♯

Third: G♯

Root: E

V   VII

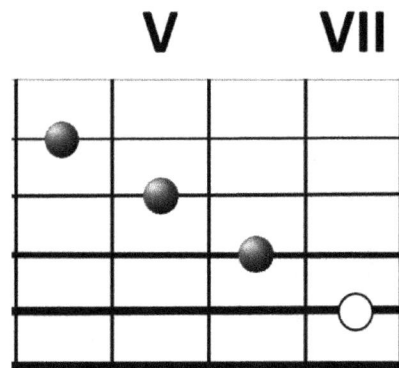

Musicians would run the world out of pens and pencils if they were to write out every single word for every single chord. A rather efficient shorthand has been developed for modern music notation; examples of the most common chord notations are as follows:

Diminished: $^{\circ}$ (E$^{\circ}$)

Minor: m, $\overline{m}$, $^{-}$ (Em, E$\overline{m}$, E^{-})

Major: No Change, Maj (E, EMaj)

Augmented: Aug, + (EAug, E+)

Fully Diminished Seven: $^{\circ 7}$ (E$^{\circ 7}$)

Half Diminished Seven: $^{\emptyset 7}$ (E$^{\emptyset 7}$)

Minor Seven: $\overline{m}^{7}$, $^{-7}$ (E$\overline{m}^{7}$, E^{-7})

Major Seven: $^{\triangle 7}$ (E$^{\triangle 7}$)

Augmented Seven: +7 (E+7)

Think of playing chords like making a bowl of cereal. Each note is an ingredient. The important thing to remember is that you use the right ingredients, not that you use them in the right order. You can add the cereal then the milk, or pour the milk then add the cereal (which is of course madness), but either way you have a bowl of cereal. The same principle applies to chords. A chord can have duplicate thirds (extra milk), or duplicate fifths (extra cereal), but you're still essentially building a bigger bowl of the same cereal. The fretboard offers plenty of notes in various locations, why not take advantage and build a bunch of different bowls with different ratios of milk to cereal? The concept of building the same chord across multiple fretboard regions is known as **chord voicing**. Voicing chords across the whole fretboard takes full advantage of all the colors and timbres that the guitar has to offer, and is a technique every developing guitarist should familiarize themselves with.

Below are three voicings for the same G major chord spread across different areas on the fretboard. Again, the objective here is to focus on texture and timbre. Does one voicing sound more full or deep? Does another sound more thin or brilliant? Really focus on the *ratios* and *ranges* of roots, thirds, and fifths, and keep these ideas in mind when moving on to concepts like inversions and the CAGED system. More on that later.

Third Position

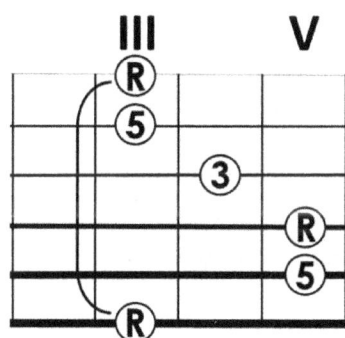

Fifth Position

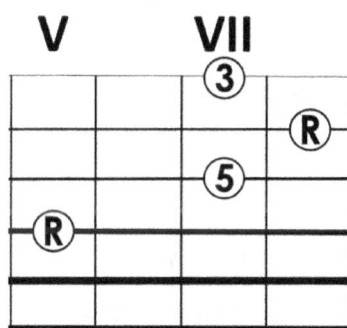

Seventh Position

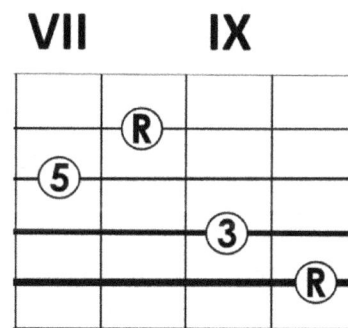

ADDITIONS, SUSPENSIONS, AND EXTENSIONS

If you are somewhat of an intermediate guitarist, I'd be willing to bet that at some point you've looked up a song, come across some strange chord like a C#min11(♭13), then mentally checked out and went straight back to playing the easy stuff for the 100th time. We've all been there, and this section is for you. Modifying chords and giving them fancy names is just another color on the artist's palette board, why not use it every once in a while? As with most things in music it's about taste; exceptional artists can do more with a single color than mediocre artists can do with an entire color wheel. It's important to understand the technique, then focus on where and when to use it.

Chord Additions are a great way to keep the primary function of a chord within a phrase, but add a level of interest that would otherwise be absent. To play an "add" chord, simply start with the original triad (root, third, fifth), then add the specified chord tone. For example, a Cadd9 chord would include the original major triad C-E-G, then add a D an octave above the root note. Remember that a 9 is a compound interval, which means its register is an octave higher in relation to the root or starting note. See page 4 for a refresher on compound intervals.

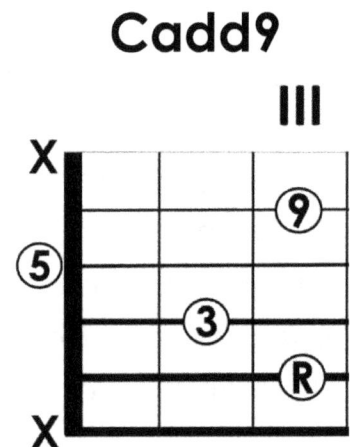

Cadd9

III

The most common "add" notes are add2, add4, add6, add9, and add11. Each of these notes default to the major spacing (M2, M4, M6, M9, and M11), and can be modified with sharps or flats to reach any desired chromatic pitch. Notes added in the same octave as the root tend to add a cluster or dissonance to the lower register, whereas notes added above the octave (compound intervals) are quite clear and provide a distinct character. You may also see add6 chords as "(note)6" (ex. C6), but the concept remains the same.

Chord Suspensions (sus chords) provide a significant amount of tension (<u>sus</u>pense) that needs to be released, usually in the following chord. The two primary sus chords are sus2 and sus4, both of which simply omit the third of the chord to create an open, unresolved sound. For instance, a Csus4 would tell us to take the original triad (C-E-G) and replace the major third with a perfect fourth from the root (C-F-G). In the vast majority of resolutions, the fourth will step down (or the second up) to resolve to the third.

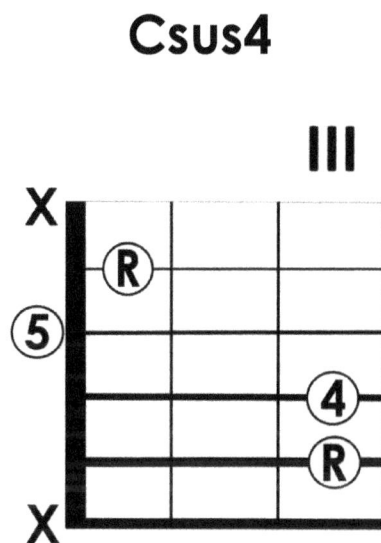

Csus4

III

Chord Extensions are very similar to additions, with a few extra notes taken into account. Whereas "add" chords only include the original triad plus one specified note, extended chords technically include the original triad plus *all* thirds up to the extension. For example, a C11 chord would include the original triad (C-E-G), plus the dominant 7 (B♭), plus the 9th (D), plus the 11th (F). In other words, a C11 chord could technically be notated as C7add9add11, but nobody's got time for that. The challenge with chord extensions is that there are often more notes to play than we have fingers, meaning some note(s) will need to be omitted, even though they are technically still part of the chord.

The most common note to remove is the fifth, as it provides little value in terms of chord quality. For 11 and 13 extensions, the next most common notes to remove are notes between the 7th and the extension. A C11 chord (C-E-G-B♭-D-F) is just as effective with the fifth and ninth removed (C-E-B♭-F), and if anything sounds more focused and less "muddy". The root can also be removed in a band context, as the bass player most likely has it handled.

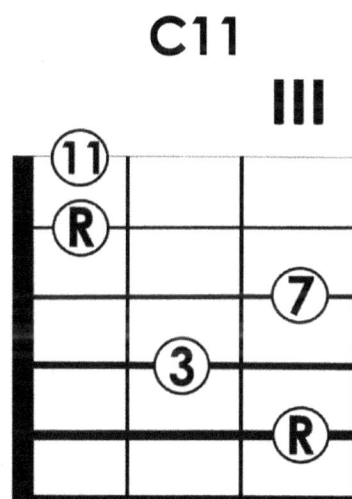

C11

III

The beauty of shorthand music notation is consolidating massive amounts of information into just a few characters, but the curse is knowing what those few characters imply when they appear in context. Shorthand is a powerful tool when used correctly, but is often misunderstood or misused. Here are some general rules when dissecting complicated clusters:

$$\textbf{C\#min7add11(b13)}$$

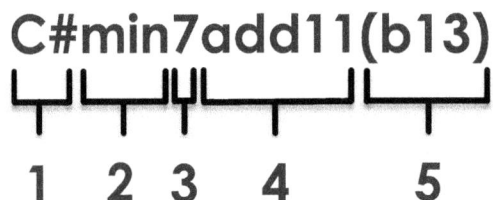

1 2 3 4 5

1: Starting note (root note)

2: Triad quality description, if absent default to major triad

3: Seventh above the root, takes quality from triad description(**2**)

> -If triad description (**2**) is diminished or minor, seventh is lowered by one half step

> -If triad description (**2**) is absent, the chord is to be read as a dominant seven, where the seventh is lowered by one half step

> -If major or augmented, seventh defaults to major spacing (M7)

> -If seventh is absent, do not play it unless otherwise implied by a higher extension (9,11, or 13)

4: Any additional note to be played within or above the octave (usually "add" or "sus" modifications)

5: Any specified notes to be raised or lowered that do NOT follow the default major spacing (usually sharp or flat extensions)

The example chord above is practically useless, but is a great example of how shorthand can be used to imply larger chords. The notation above would imply the notes C#-E-G#-B-D#-F#-A.

INVERSIONS

As we discovered in the chord qualities and voicings section, the important part of playing a chord is using the right notes, not necessarily using the notes in the same *order*. Adding more milk to your cereal is fine, but if you add orange juice you're gonna have a bad time. The same is true when it comes to the concept of inversions. An **inversion** is simply a re-arrangement of the notes in a chord so that a note other than the root is on the bottom. Notes in the middle or top of the chord can be voiced in any order, but the inversion is still classified by which note from the chord is in the bass (bottom). A root in the bass is classified as **root position**, a third in the bass is a **first inversion**, a fifth in the bass is classified as a **second inversion**, and a seventh in the bass is a **third inversion**.

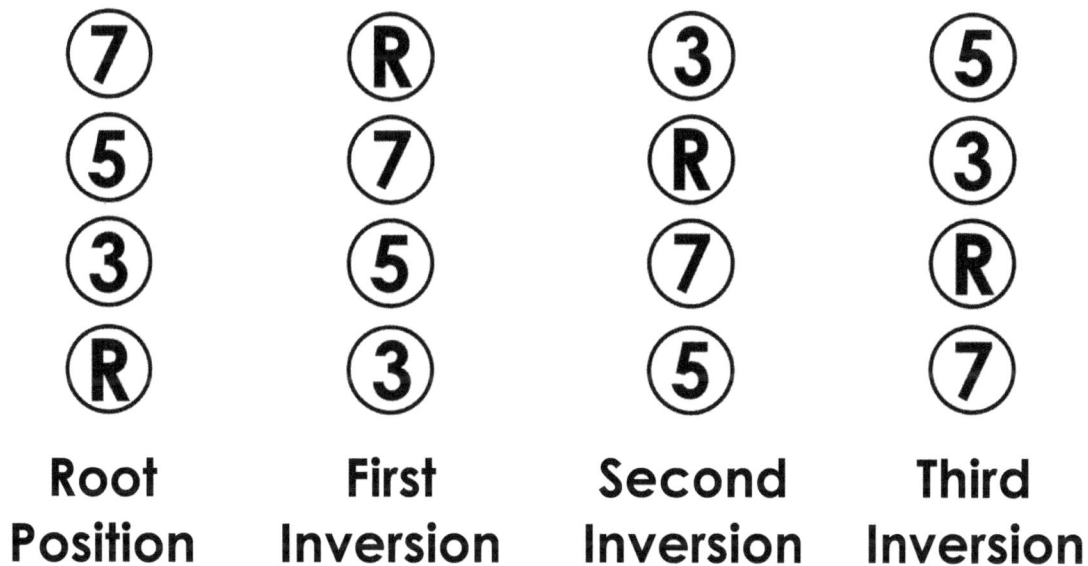

Root Position	First Inversion	Second Inversion	Third Inversion

Because notes of the same chord can be found across the fretboard, we can group them together to make inversions. The following diagrams are examples of the four primary chord qualities inverted across the fretboard. Keep in mind these diagrams are relative to the root note represented by the open circles, and can be shifted any number of frets to start on any desired root note.

Diminished Inversions

Minor Inversions

Major Inversions

Augmented Inversions

Of course, the notes in any chord can be re-shuffled across various positions on the fretboard to create new inversions. These groupings of inversions can be lined up in a row to create a consistent road map across the fretboard, where the end of one shape is the beginning of the next. This is a concept that will be elaborated on a little later in the CAGED system section. Below are some layouts for the most commonly used minor and major inversion groups.

Minor Inversion Layout

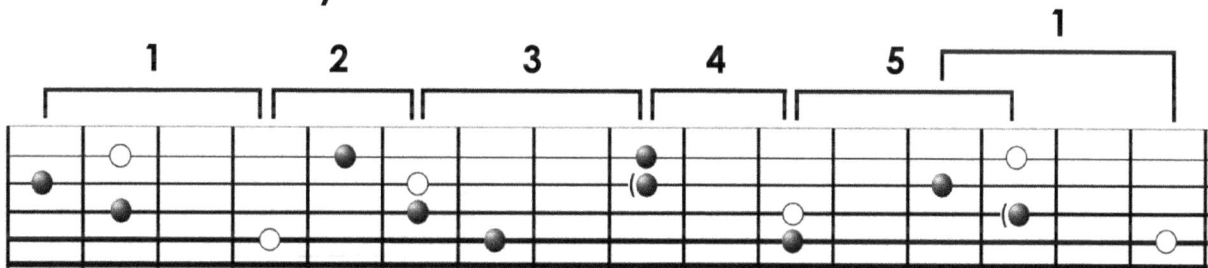

Major Inversion Layout

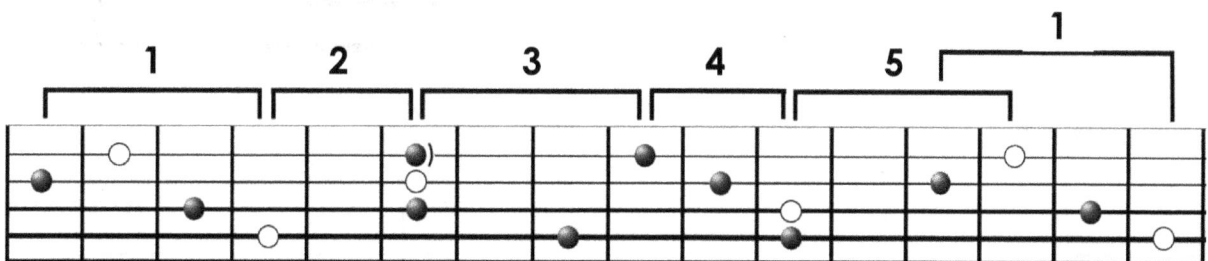

Inversions have two primary functions. The first function is to change chords while remaining in the same position on the fretboard. Rather than physically shifting locations for every chord in a passage, it may be more advantageous to remain in the same location and find inversions that fit in the same region. The second function is to add color or texture so that the guitar fits seamlessly within the larger context of a full band. Standard root position chords may sound too dark or muddy, but perhaps a first or second inversion chord provides just enough clarity that the listener can decipher the sound of the guitar above the bass. Experiment with different inversions to see what textures fit best with your overall sound.

ARPEGGIOS

The word arpeggio is derived from the Italian language, and roughly translates to "playing the harp". True to its harp-like practice, **arpeggiation** is the act of breaking up a chord and playing it one note at a time. Arpeggios lay out quite nicely on the fretboard through a three-octave system, as seen below. The following are root-third-fifth "relationships" for the four primary chord qualities. Once again, notice that there are no fret markers as each of these diagrams can be shifted to start on any desired note.

Diminished Arpeggio Layout

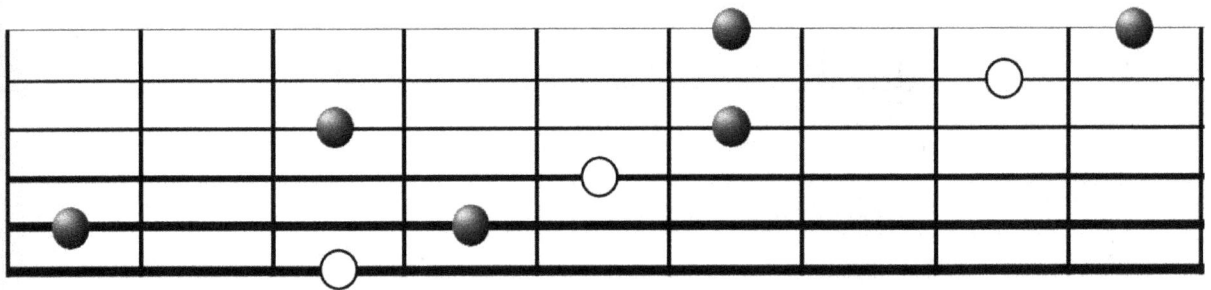

Diminished Arpeggio Layout (Alternate)

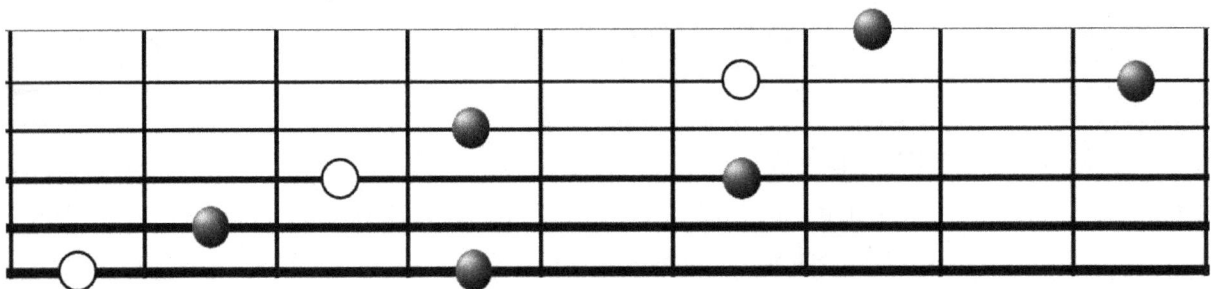

Minor Arpeggio Layout

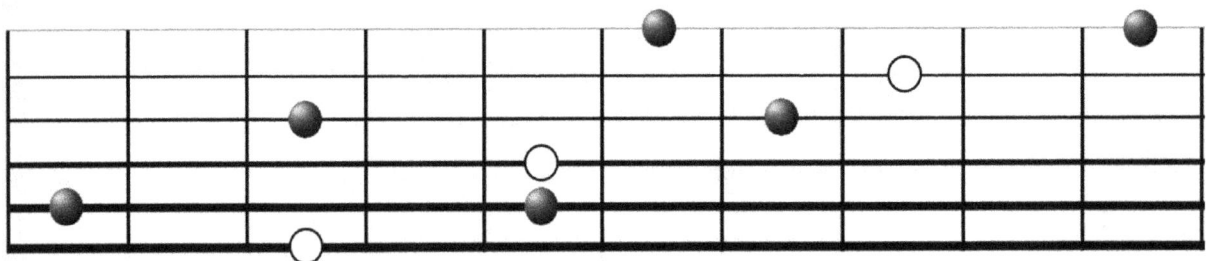

Minor Arpeggio Layout (Alternate)

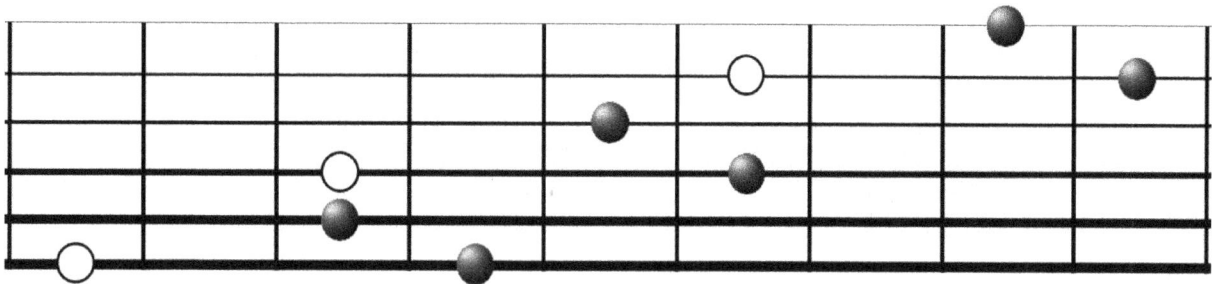

Major Arpeggio Layout

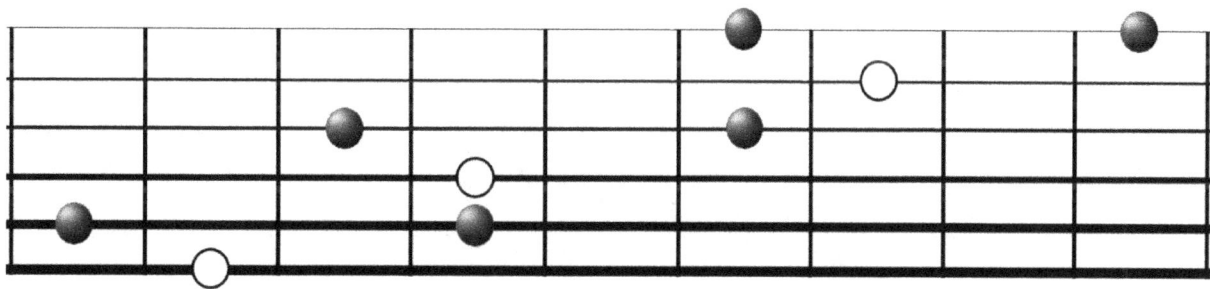

Major Arpeggio Layout (Alternate)

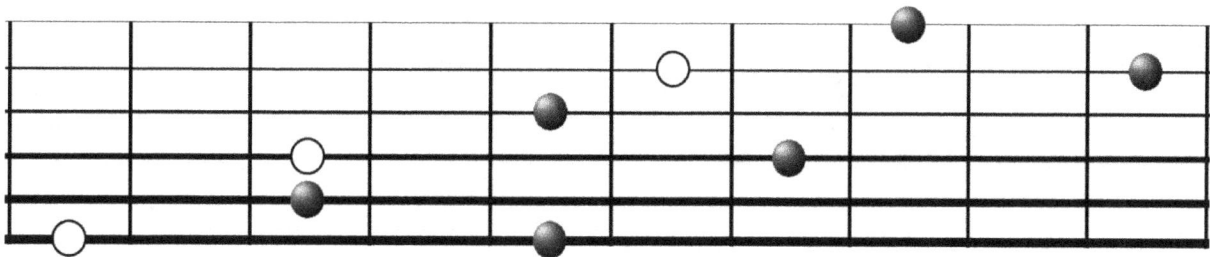

Augmented Arpeggio Layout

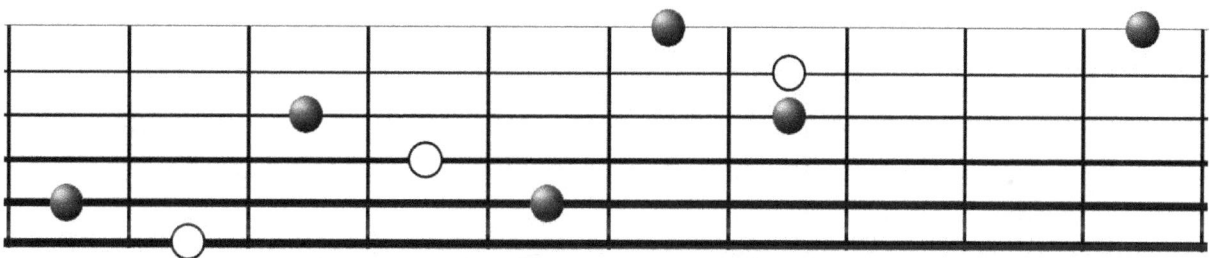

Augmented Arpeggio Layout (Alternate)

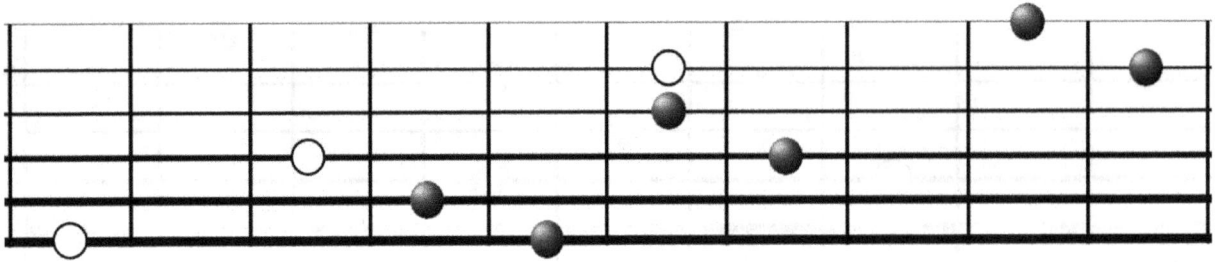

Though it is a more advanced and technically difficult arpeggio, adding the seventh provides additional color:

Minor Seven Arpeggio Layout

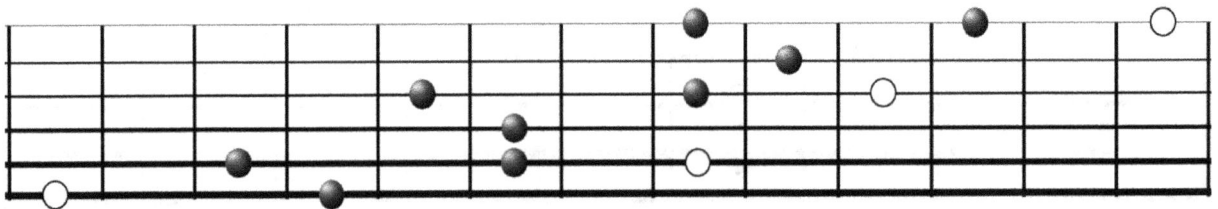

Major Seven Arpeggio Layout

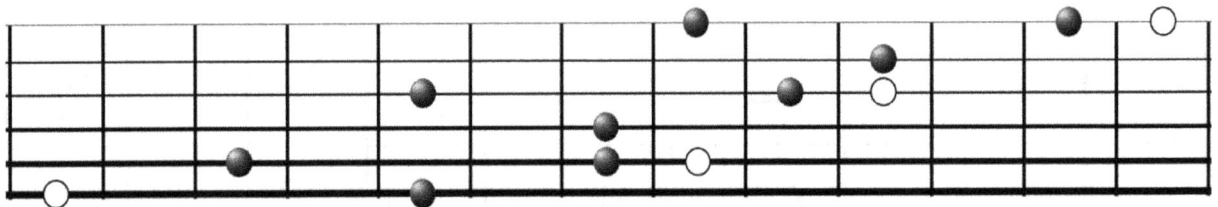

Arpeggios can also lay out over a string-skipping pattern for a more classical or piano-like sound. Augmented string skipping patterns are highly inefficient and often too far of a stretch physically, and have been omitted from the following group of diagrams for that reason.

Diminished String Skipping Layouts

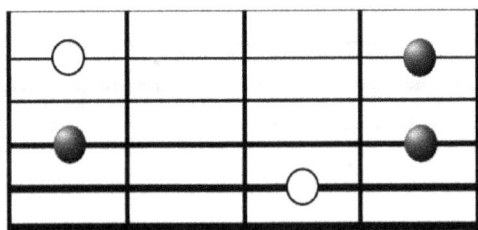

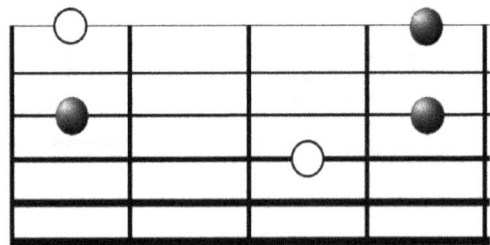

Minor String Skipping Layouts

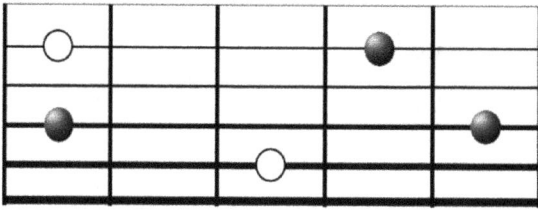

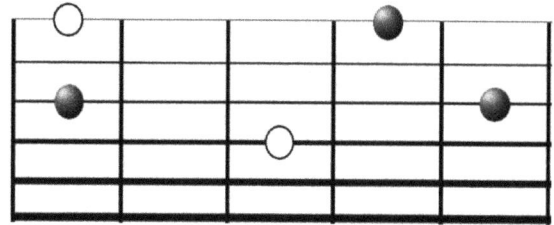

Major String Skipping Layouts

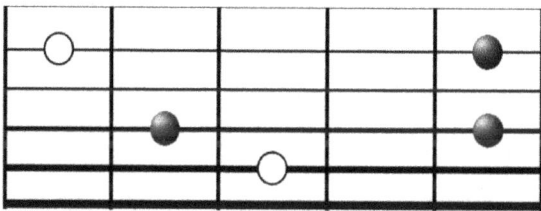

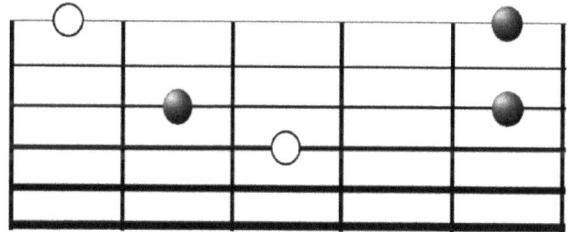

Arpeggios are a great way to travel across the fretboard at high speeds, and are often used to create momentum and direction. They are the hammer to every developing guitarist's toolbox, although one should use caution when swinging. Strike at the right time in the right place and people will think you're a genius. Strike at everything everywhere and people will see you as "that guy" who has great technique but lacks awareness or feel. Just because you are really good at swinging a hammer, doesn't mean everything becomes a nail. Arpeggios are excellent for elevating a solo or guitar part to a higher level, and if used in *just* the right spot can send an otherwise mediocre solo into overdrive. As with everything in guitar theory, experiment and draw your own conclusions as to when the technique is best used in your personal vocabulary.

HARMONY IN THIRDS AND SIXTHS

Understanding harmony is a key step to developing a good musical ear, as harmonization plays a key role in building upon chords and melodies. Harmonies of thirds and sixths are most common, as seconds and sevenths are quite dissonant, and fourths and fifths provide little value in terms of chord quality or character. To **harmonize** in thirds, simply play two scale degrees from the major scale that are a third apart. These relationships are scale degrees 1 and 3, 2 and 4, 3 and 5, 4 and 6, 5 and 7, 6 and 1, and 7 and 2. Some of these interval relationships will be minor thirds, and others will be major. The following diagrams represent relationships in thirds between adjacent strings, and can be shifted to any desired starting fret. The dotted lines match the scales degrees to their harmonized third within the major scale. The open diamonds represent the scale's minor starting point (scale degree 6) in relation to the major (scale degree 1) starting point on the open circles.

Thirds on the E and A Strings

Thirds on the A and D Strings

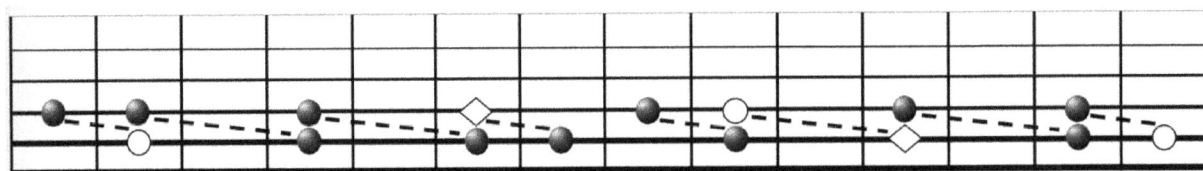

Thirds on the D and G Strings

Thirds on the G and B Strings

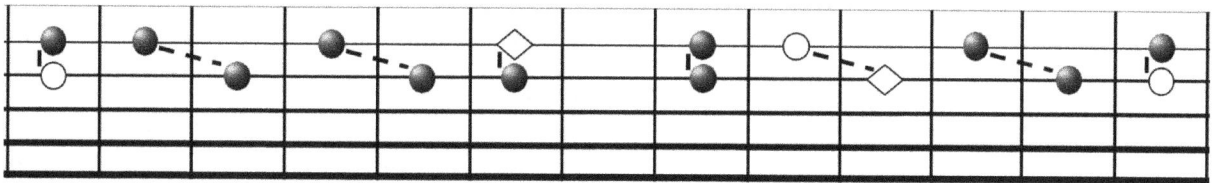

Thirds on the B and E Strings

The same approach applies to harmony in sixths. Another way to think of harmony in sixths is to play a note within the major scale that is a sixth above your starting note. These relationships exist between scale degrees 1 and 6, 2 and 7, 3 and 1, 4 and 2, 5 and 3, 6 and 4, and 7 and 5.

Sixths on the E and D Strings

Sixths on the A and G Strings

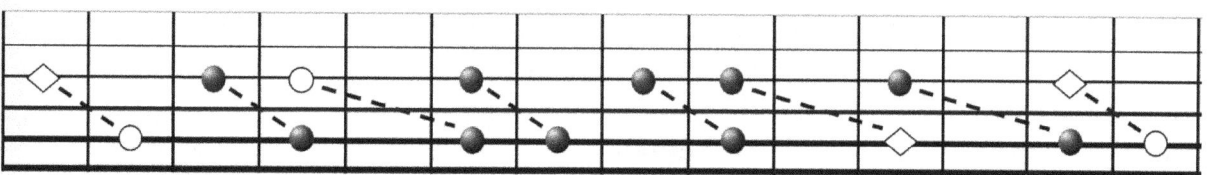

Sixths on the D and B Strings

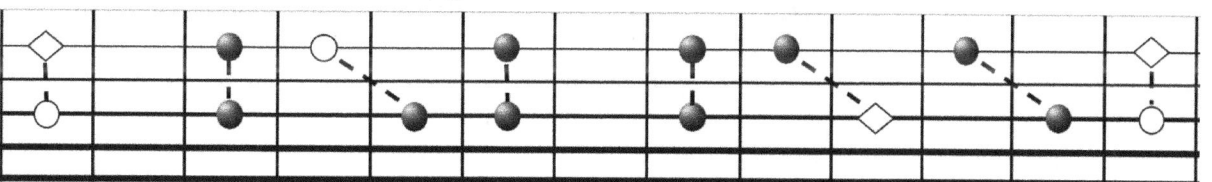

Sixths on the G and E Strings

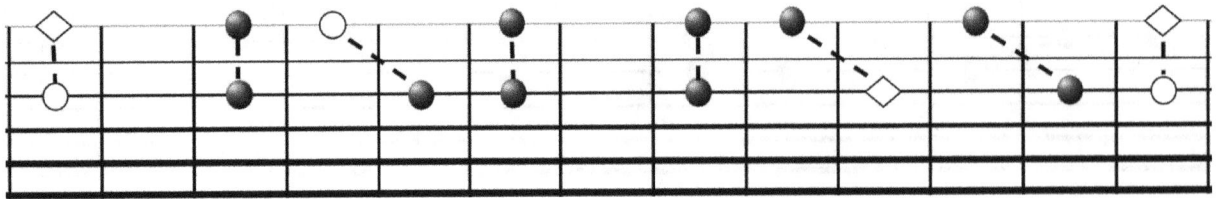

You may notice that these layouts on the fretboard are somewhat similar. That is because thirds and sixths are related to one another from a theory standpoint. If you lower your third by one octave, the result is a sixth between the lowered note and the root note. Similarly, lowering the sixth by an octave will result in a third below the root note. The same concept applies to the relationship between seconds and sevenths, fourths and fifths, and technically unisons and octaves.

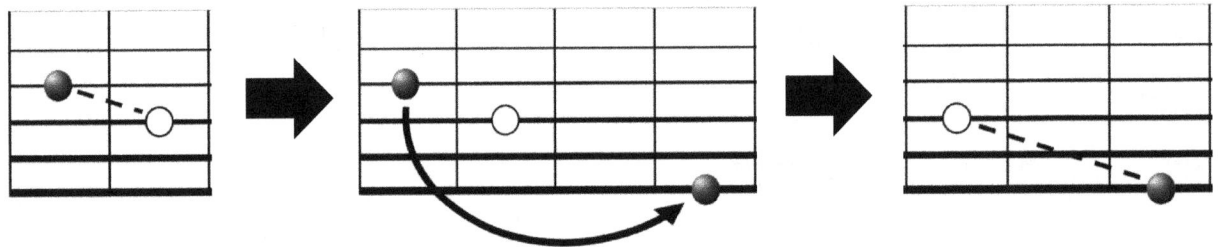

Major Third   **Harmony Down One Octave**   **Minor Sixth**

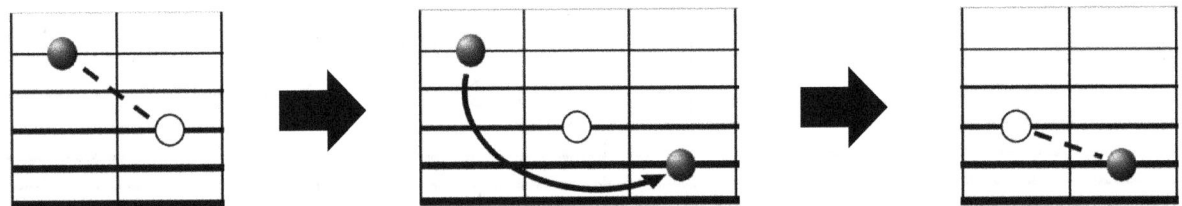

Minor Sixth   **Harmony Down One Octave**   **Major Third**

These relationships exist all over the fretboard, and open the door to endless harmonic possibilities. When in doubt, *harmonize*.

THE CAGED SYSTEM AND ITS VARIANTS

The CAGED system plays a fundamental role in fretboard visualization. Once understood, the CAGED system illuminates the entire reasoning behind standard tuning and pattern navigation. It can be used to find any chord in any key at any given location on the fretboard. Mastery of this theoretical approach will result in the ability to fit into the vast majority of musical settings and provide a visual foundation to build off of. The diagrams below represent the five main shapes of the CAGED system. Each shape corresponds to its letter, and therefore its relationship to the other shapes within the system. The open diagrams are played on the first three frets using open strings, while the closed diagrams are fully-fretted and can be moved around from position to position.

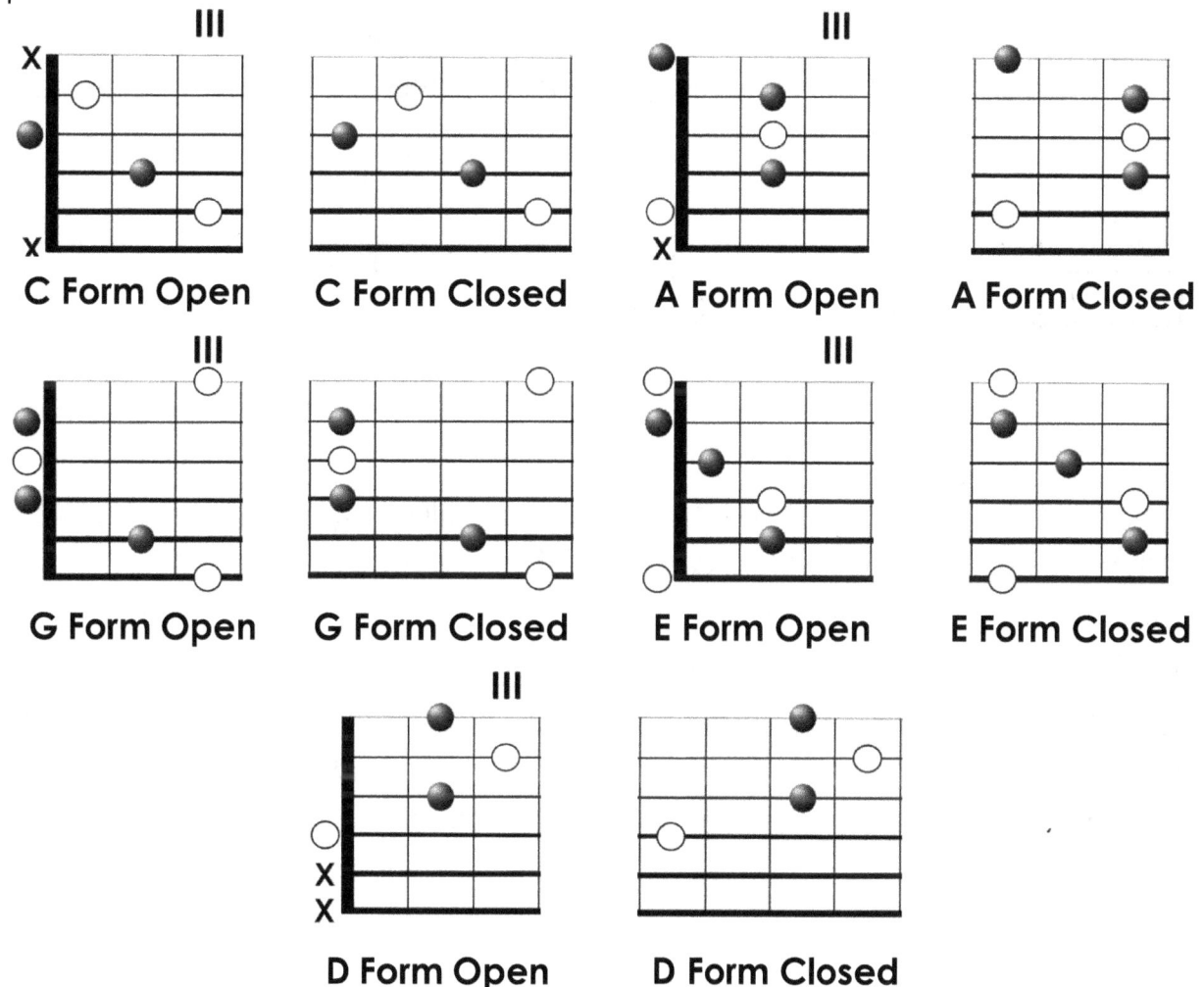

C Form Open	C Form Closed	A Form Open	A Form Closed
G Form Open	G Form Closed	E Form Open	E Form Closed
D Form Open	D Form Closed		

The CAGED system receives its name from a very specific arrangement of chord shapes. Each shape is linked, where the end of one is the beginning of the next. Keep in mind that while the *shape* changes, the *quality* of the chord remains the same. For example, a CAGED system with a root on C will produce five different C Major chords across the fretboard:

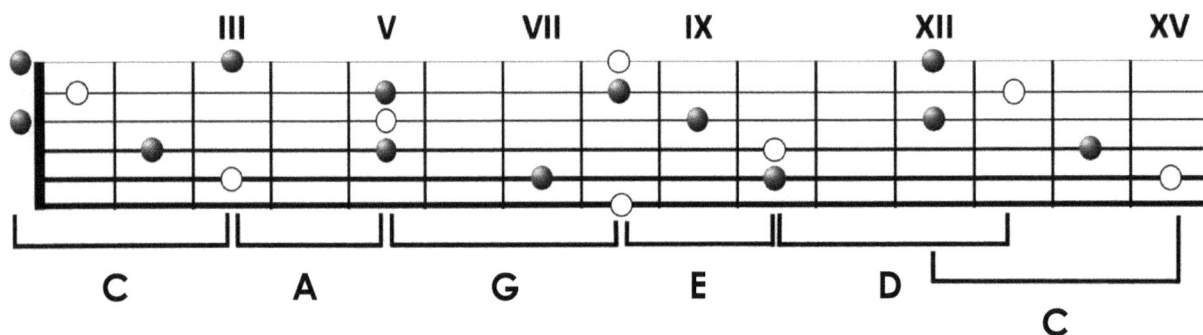

To change chords, the entire system can be shifted across any number of frets. Continuing on the example above, the entire "network" can shift up two frets to produce five linked D Major chords:

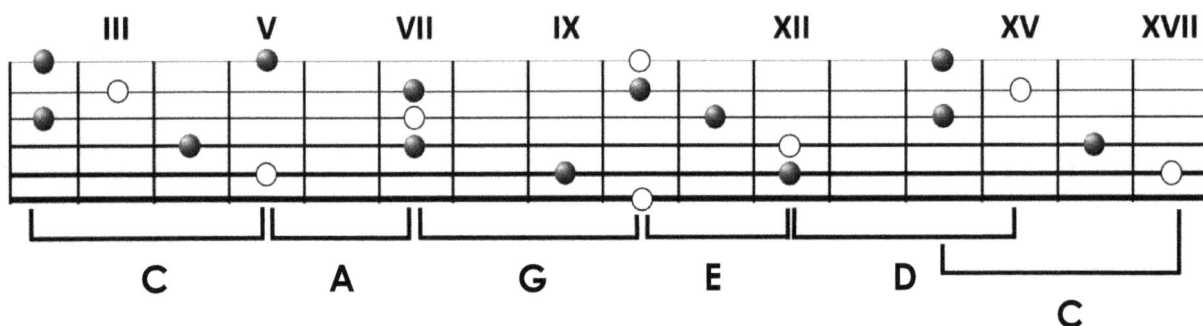

Because the system is a theoretical endless loop, you can start anywhere on the fretboard and work backwards or forwards until you run out of frets. When using the CAGED system, the objective is to visualize each shape and the connection points between them. The goal is not to run around doing "mental gymnastics" on the fretboard, but instead to develop the ability to immediately access a range of timbres and registers that can color your sound in a variety of ways.

Beyond color and timbre diversity, the CAGED system also provides a significant physical advantage when switching between chords. Rather than shifting from position to position when changing chords, the CAGED system localizes voicings to allow the left hand to remain in place relative to the neck. For example, let's say we want to dabble with the chords E minor, G major, A minor, and B Major. Each of these chords *could* be played in their open positions, but for argument's sake let's say there's another guitarist already covering that. How can we add another level of texture to contribute to the sound? We could slide all over the neck and lose our sense of stability and consistency, *or* we could use the CAGED system to keep everything tight and focused in a localized range:

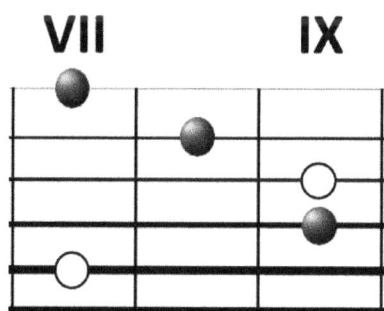

E Minor (A Form)

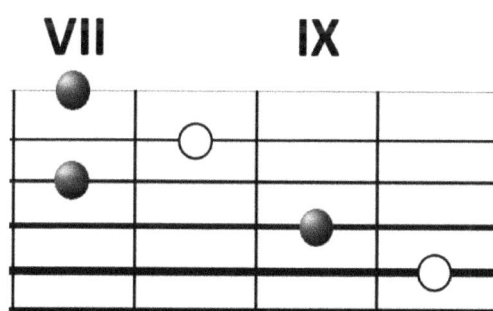

G Major (C Form)

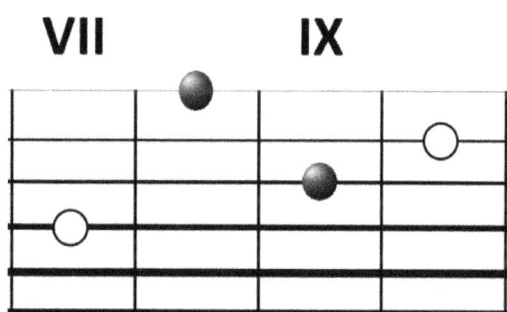

A Minor (D Form)

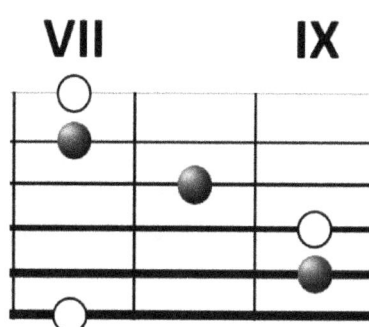

B Major (E Form)

Using the voicings above, all four chords can be played in seventh position without the inefficiencies of shifting to new locations. There is always a CAGED solution when switching between chords, all you have to do is look for it!

The **Pentatonic CAGED System** fills in two more notes within each octave, producing five principal pentatonic shapes or "boxes". Once again, the open diamonds represent the relative minor starting note (6th scale degree) in relation to the Major (1st scale degree) starting note.

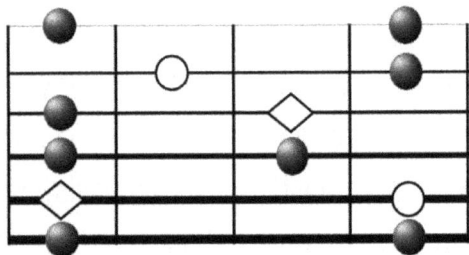

C Form

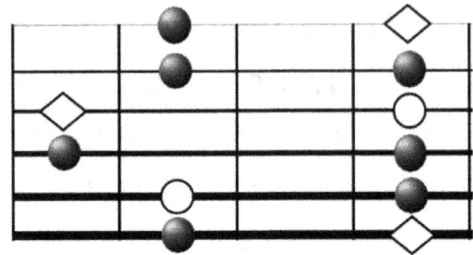

A Form

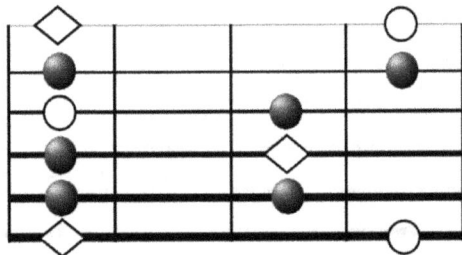

G Form

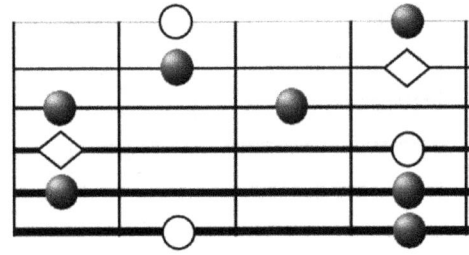

E Form

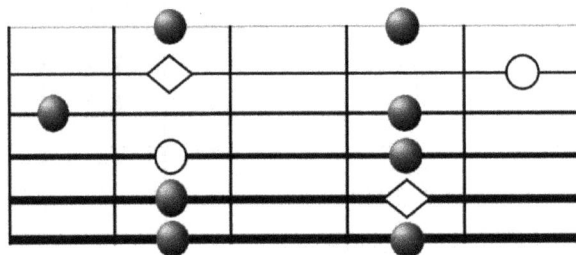

D Form

While it is easy to learn one or two pentatonic boxes and call it a day, I would highly recommend familiarizing yourself with all five shapes. This is the kind of material that takes a guitarist from melodic infancy and develops them into a unique player that has found their own voice. Find the dots and connect away!

Similar to the original CAGED shapes, each one of these scale variations connect to the next, creating a seamless loop starting anywhere on the fretboard. These interconnected shapes are quite useful for constructing solos and filling in lead lines.

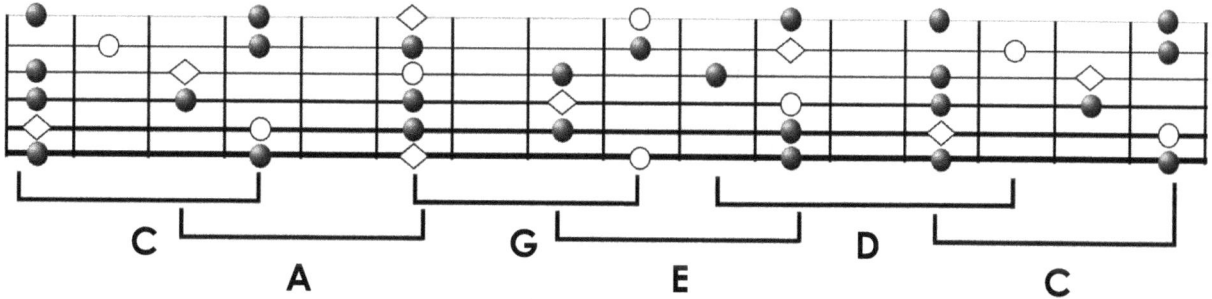

The addition of the **blue note** (flat 3 in relation to the major root and flat 5 in relation to the minor) gives us the blues scale. These patterns are great for lead licks and adding a little bit of spice to an otherwise bland solo. The blue note is generally treated as a **passing tone**, meaning that the note is played between two stable tones and suggests a subtle sense of chromaticism. As with all techniques, try to use it with taste. A little goes a long way when it comes to chromatic embellishments. The blue note is represented by the open squares in the following diagrams.

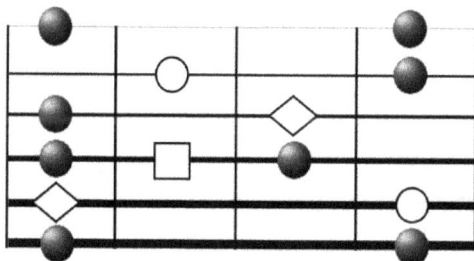

C Form With Blue Note

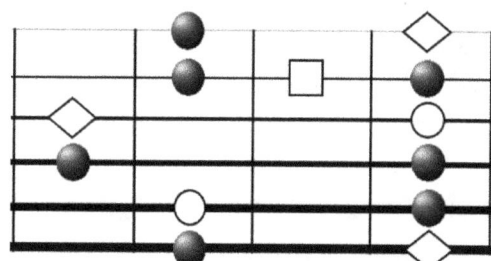

A Form With Blue Note

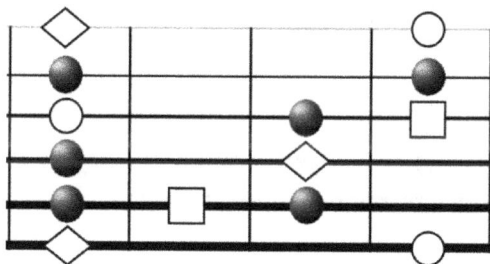

G Form With Blue Note

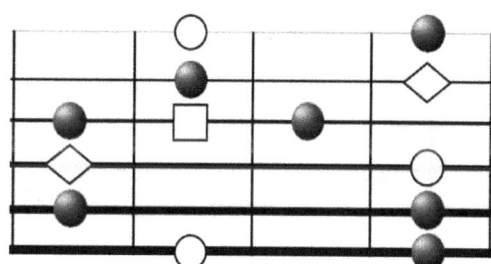

E Form With Blue Note

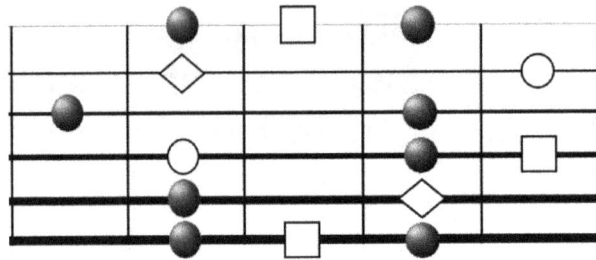

D Form With Blue Note

Once again, each of the CAGED shapes can be joined together to provide a consistent "road map" across the fretboard.

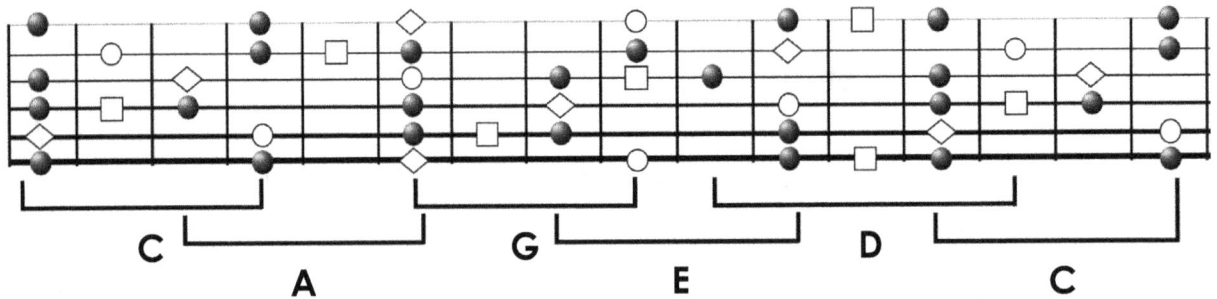

C   A   G   E   D   C

The **Diatonic CAGED System** follows all the previous directives, this time the fourth and seventh scale degrees have been added to complete the diatonic scale. This is the final form of the CAGED system.

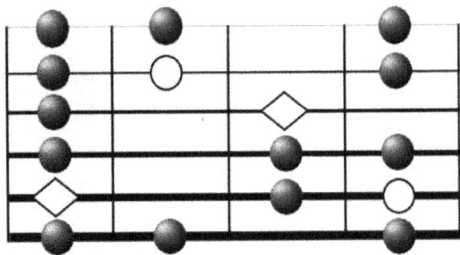

Diatonic C Form

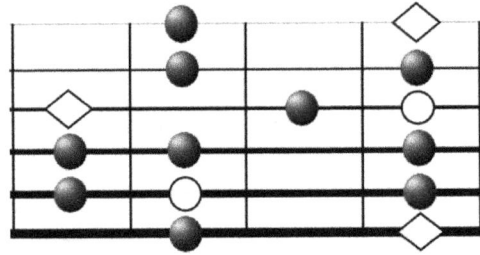

Diatonic A Form

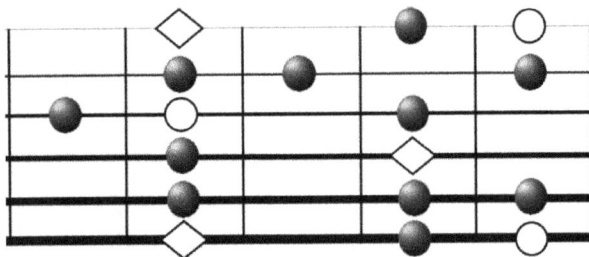

Diatonic G Form

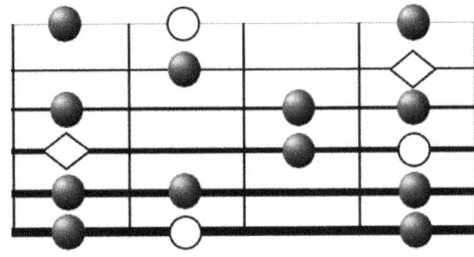

Diatonic E Form

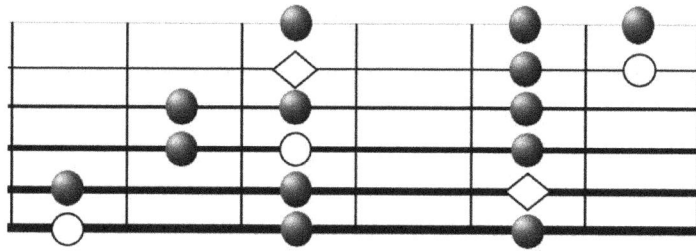

Diatonic D Form

Memorization of this final diatonic "road map" will allow you to travel anywhere across the fretboard with complete control and understanding of where you are and where you are going. This material will help you navigate any key in any context, and essentially tells you *what* to say. All that's left for you to decide is *when and how* you say it.

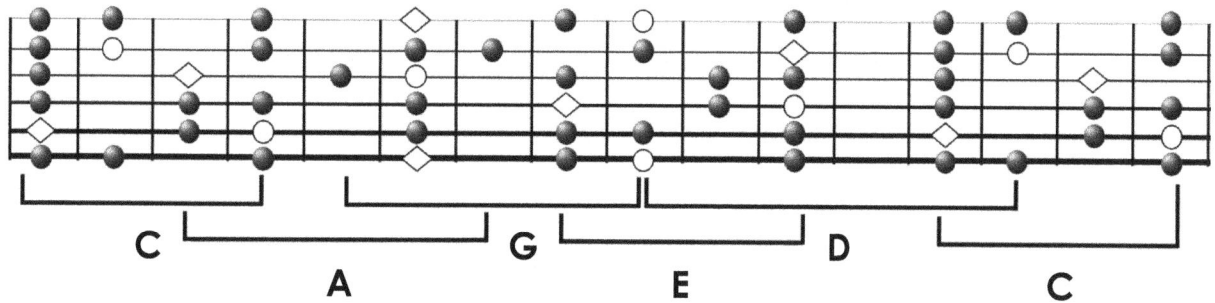

A brief word of warning on the CAGED system. When used appropriately, it is a beautiful network capable of cutting an overwhelming amount of information into digestible bite-sized pieces. The problem arises when players memorize these shapes and play them linearly with no sense of melodic hierarchy or phrasing. That is not making music; that's playing scales over a band. Time and again, guitarists make the mistake of playing what they *see*, and not what they *hear*. This results in hours of chart memorization only to go searching online for lessons on how to "break out of the box". These shapes and systems should be used as a visual reference for fretboard navigation, but ultimately give way to the player's ear. Some of the most lyrical and melodic playing comes from the most uncomfortable and nonsensical physical layouts on the fretboard.

These lead pattern variants are a great example of transcending the system positions and following your ear for some killer lead runs.

Lead Pattern 1

Lead Pattern 2

Lead Pattern 3

Lead Pattern 4

THE THREE NOTE PER STRING (3NPS) SYSTEM

The CAGED system is a vital tool for navigation across the fretboard in any key, but it reaches a breaking point when it comes to speed. The majority of CAGED system shapes have one string that only has two notes from the diatonic scale on it, creating a slight mental and physical "stumble" when moving through the shape at high speeds. Enter the **Three Note Per String System**, conceptually redesigned for ergonomics and physical efficiency. This is how the hot shots shred 300 notes per minute with a fluid-like execution. As the name suggests, each string within a given form has three notes from the diatonic scale. There is no interruption between movements from string to string, and the timing can be perfectly synchronized. Proper execution of 3NPS shapes will result in a more fluid and even sound from note to note. There are seven 3NPS forms, one for each scale degree of the diatonic scale.

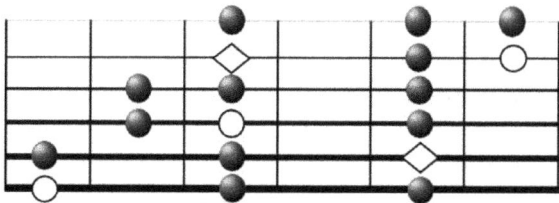

Form 1

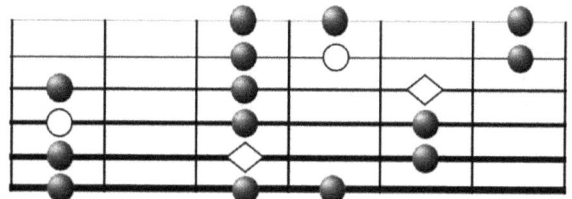

Form 2

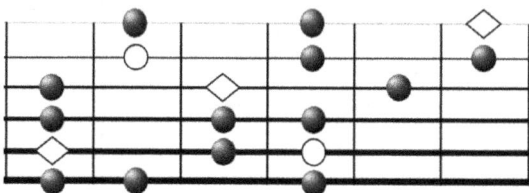

Form 3

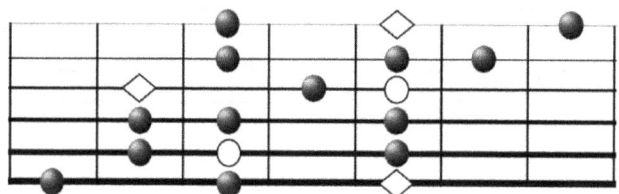

Form 4

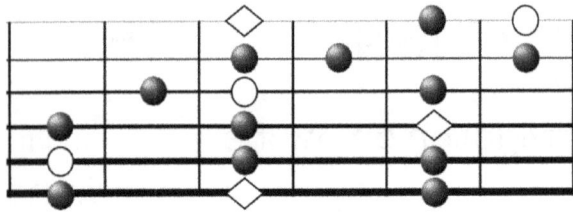

Form 5

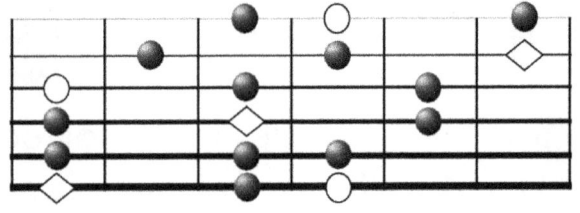

Form 6

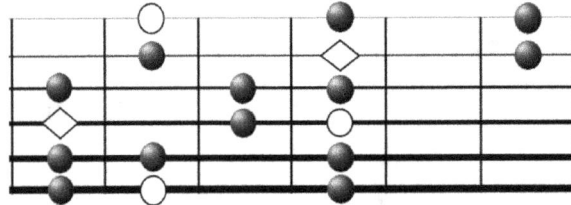

Form 7

Just like the CAGED system, each form of the 3NPS system can be tied together to make one complete collage across the fretboard. The entire system can then be moved up or down any desired number of frets to change the key. Once again, the Major key is represented by the open circles (scale degree 1) and the relative minor is represented by the open diamonds (scale degree 6).

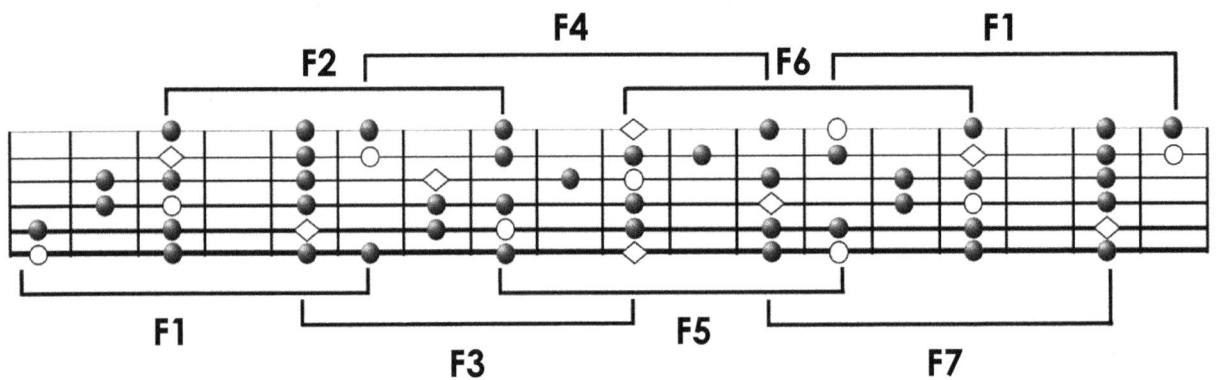

MODES

For no reason at all, many guitarists tend to think that modes are this obscure trophy that you have to sell your soul and unlock your seventh chakra to understand. Yes, there are a few "rules" and patterns to wrap your head around, but it's the same process as any other musical idea. Input, process, practice, repeat. Most of the confusion and obscurity come from the fact that you can look up "modes for guitar" and get seven different explanations from seven different people who understand modes seven different ways. There are multiple ways to get to the same answer here, all that matters is that YOU understand the end result. For this reason, I'll include an FAQ section followed by three different (but equally valid) methods to go about navigating the modes.

What is a mode?

A **mode** is simply a re-organization of the notes in a specified scale so that a different scale degree is prioritized as the starting note (tonic). Each of these re-organizations will have their own color and emotion, just like the different scales presented in the scales section on page 8.

How many modes are there?

There are seven traditional modes (also known as church modes), one for each scale degree of the major scale. While it is possible to re-organize scales other than the major scale, it is highly uncommon to see in theory and even less common to hear in modern music. 99.99% of music with modes will use the seven traditional modes based off the major scale. Each mode has a specific name and order, which automatically tells the player what specific notes to play, and what note to prioritize as the tonic. The names and order of the modes are as follows:

Mode Number (Order)	Mode Name	Scale Degree From Major Scale Prioritized	Mode Quality
1	Ionian	1	Major
2	Dorian	2	Minor
3	Phrygian	3	Minor
4	Lydian	4	Major
5	Mixolydian	5	Major
6	Aeolean	6	Minor
7	Locrian	7	Minor

What makes a mode major or minor (mode quality)?

While each of the seven modes have their own unique sound and emotion, they are generally categorized as major or minor "ish", depending on the interval from the mode's tonic to its third. If the distance from the tonic to the third is a major third, the mode is major. If the interval is minor, the mode is minor. This places Ionian, Lydian, and Mixolydian in the "major" category, and Dorian, Phrygian, Aeolean, and Locrian in the "minor" category. There is some academic debate as to whether the Locrian mode is truly a minor mode, or if it deserves its own category as the only diminished mode. The mode itself is used in context so sparingly that the argument itself is somewhat inconsequential.

What's the point of modes and how do I use them?

Modes are just another color on the artist's palette board. They are most effective when used in prominent lines like melodies or guitar solos, but can really be used anywhere from small licks to entire songs.

How do I know what notes are in a given mode?

Well, that's just the trick. Having been in both the student's and teacher's seat, here are the three most common ways I have seen modes taught and organized:

Method 1: The Intervallic Approach

As stated previously, modes are a re-organization of the major scale, which is just a bunch of half-steps and whole-steps put together. The specific order of half-steps and whole-steps for the major scale is as follows, where H represents a half-step and W represents a whole-step:

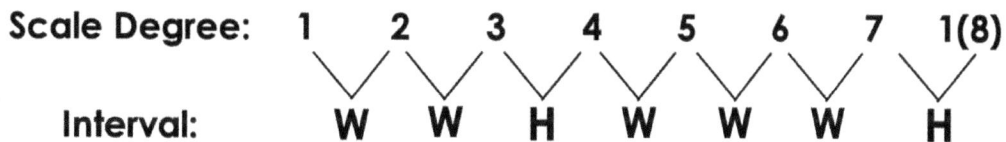

Scale Degree: 1   2   3   4   5   6   7   1(8)

Interval: W   W   H   W   W   W   H

This combination of half-steps and whole-steps gives us both the major scale AND our first mode. Since Ionian is synonymous with the major scale, this pattern can also be used to play the Ionian mode. The next mode (Dorian) uses the EXACT same sequence of half-steps and whole-steps, but starts on the second interval. This pushes the first whole-step to the end of the line, making the sequence W-H-W-W-W-H-W, like so:

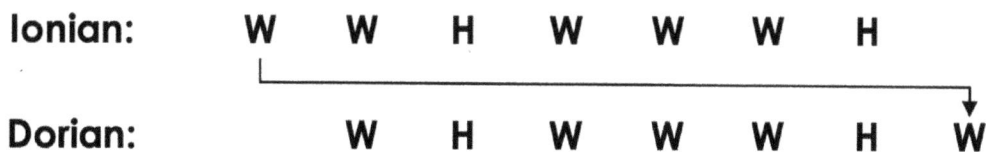

Ionian: W   W   H   W   W   W   H

Dorian: W   H   W   W   W   H   W

The third mode does the exact same thing, using the major scale sequence but starting on the third interval in the pattern, sending the first two to the back of the line:

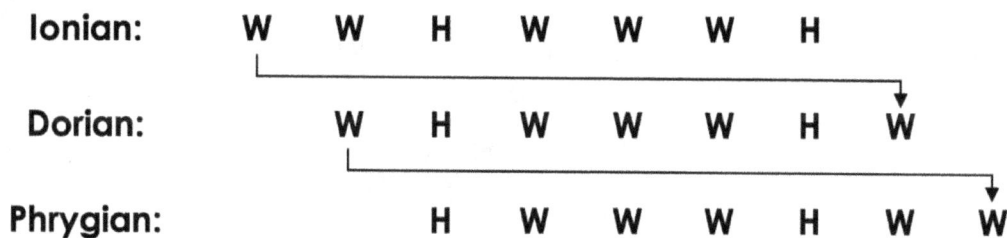

Ionian: W   W   H   W   W   W   H

Dorian: W   H   W   W   W   H   W

Phrygian: H   W   W   W   H   W   W

This pattern continues seven times over, until it shuffles itself back to the original starting interval and order. The following diagram shows the full re-shuffling of all the modes and their corresponding sequence of half-steps and whole-steps:

Ionian:	W	W	H	W	W	W	H	
Dorian:		W	H	W	W	W	H	W
Phrygian:		H	W	W	W	H	W	W
Lydian:		W	W	W	H	W	W	H
Mixolydian:		W	W	H	W	W	H	W
Aeolean:		W	H	W	W	H	W	W
Locrian:		H	W	W	H	W	W	W
Ionian:		W	W	H	W	W	W	H

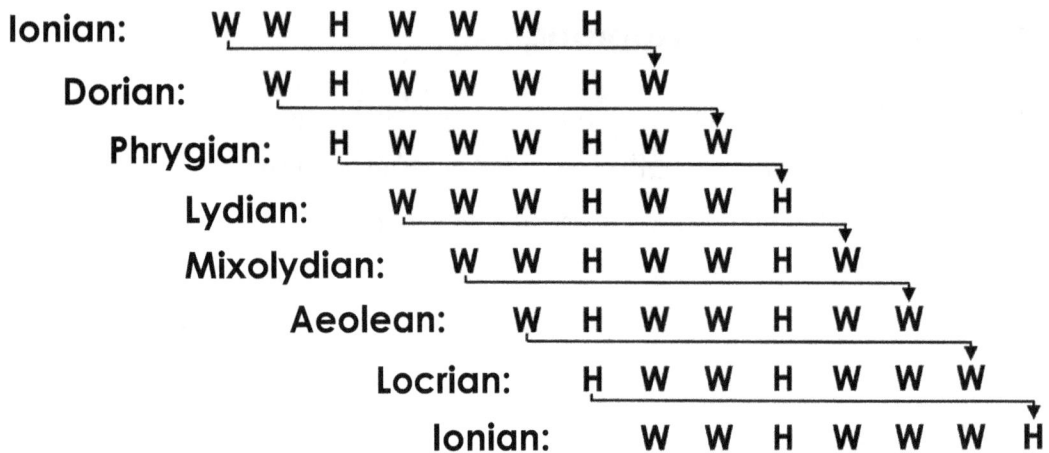

Here's the kicker: the interval sequence changes, but the starting note stays the same. For example, C Ionian and C Dorian both start on C, but they have different interval sequences. C Ionian would use the interval sequence W-W-H-W-W-W-H, where Dorian would use the sequence W-H-W-W-W-H-W, creating two entirely different groups of notes. The following diagram demonstrates this concept applied to all modes starting on the note C:

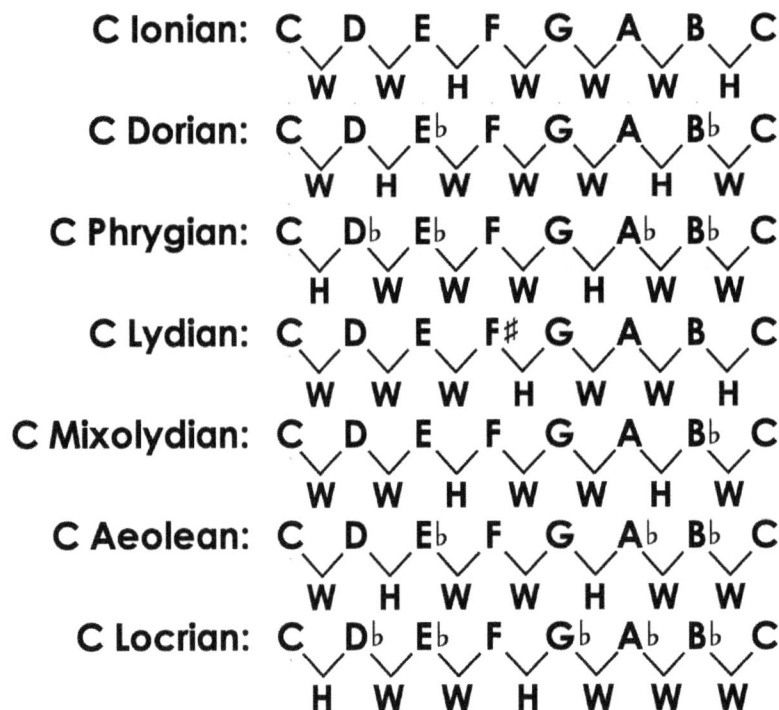

C Ionian: C D E F G A B C
W W H W W W H

C Dorian: C D E♭ F G A B♭ C
W H W W W H W

C Phrygian: C D♭ E♭ F G A♭ B♭ C
H W W W H W W

C Lydian: C D E F♯ G A B C
W W W H W W H

C Mixolydian: C D E F G A B♭ C
W W H W W H W

C Aeolean: C D E♭ F G A♭ B♭ C
W H W W H W W

C Locrian: C D♭ E♭ F G♭ A♭ B♭ C
H W W H W W W

The intervallic approach works for all modes starting on any note. Simply choose a starting note and use a specified interval sequence.

Method 2: The Parent Key Approach

The circle of fifths is your best friend when using this method. A strong foundational knowledge of key signatures and order of accidentals gives any developing guitarist immediate access to note (and therefore mode) recognition and perception. If you're not familiar with the circle of fifths, there's no time like the present.

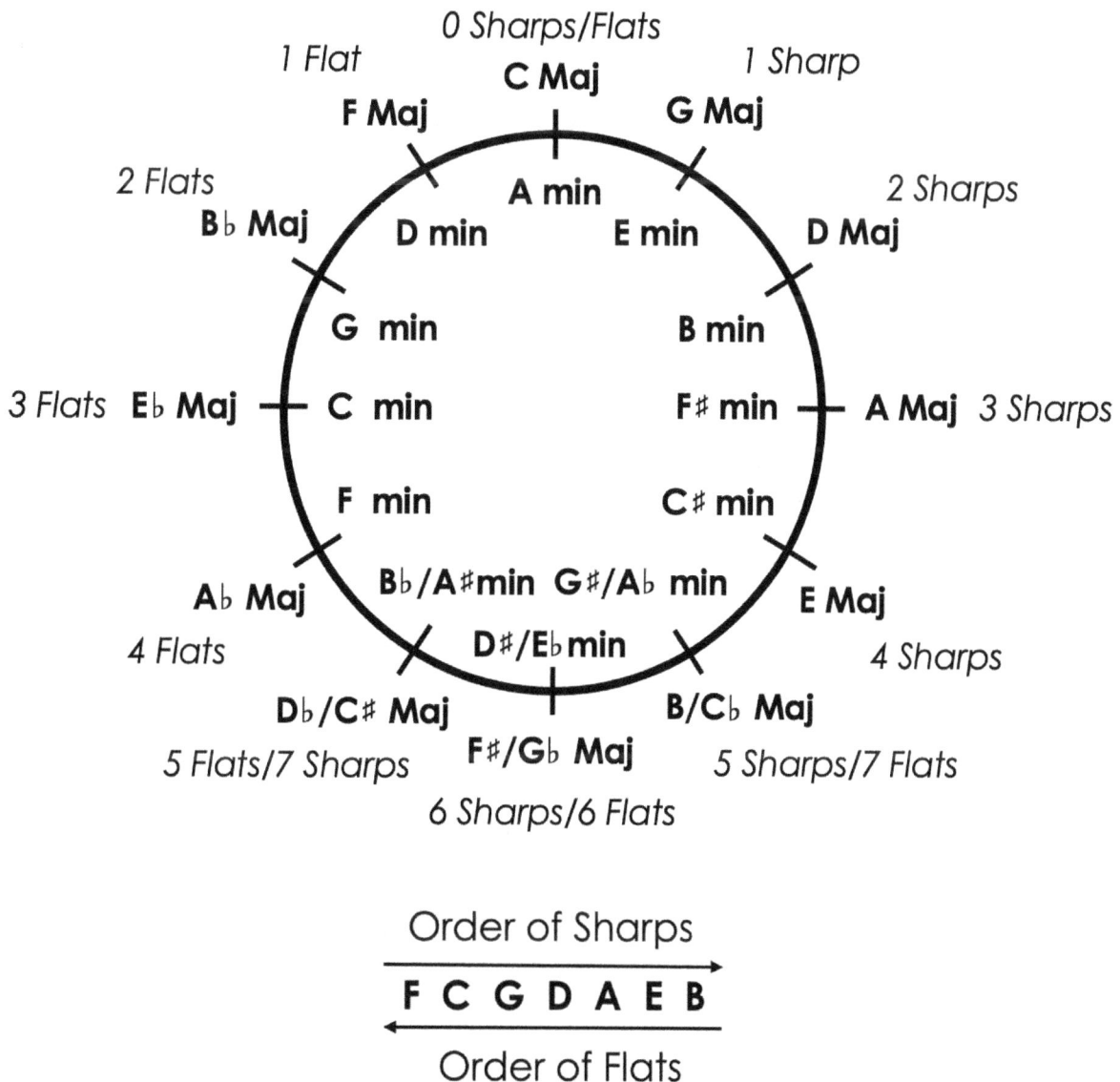

Order of Sharps

F C G D A E B

Order of Flats

While an entirely separate book could be written on the beauty and utility of the circle of fifths, here is a crash course for all you need in order to use the Parent Key approach for modes:

Each location on the circle of fifths has a corresponding number of sharps or flats. To find all the notes within a key, simply list out the seven natural notes then add the specified number of sharps or flats in their correct order. Let's find all the notes in the key of E Major:

1: List out the seven natural notes in order. Every major and minor scale has exactly seven scale degrees, and none can be skipped. That means there has to be some kind of scale degree one, some kind of scale degree two, etc... In this example, we can safely lay out the notes E through D, *then* go back and modify them with accidentals:

$$E-F-G-A-B-C-D$$

2: Referencing the circle of fifths, we see that the key of E Major has four sharps. Which sharps? The first four from the "order of sharps", which is a hard rule that will never be broken for any key signature. Therefore, we apply F♯, C♯, G♯, and D♯ in that order:

$$\overset{(1)}{E}-\overset{(3)}{F♯}-G♯-A-B-\overset{(2)}{C♯}-\overset{(4)}{D♯}$$

Poof! E Major. For the sake of example, let's do one more in the key of F minor:

1: List out the seven natural notes in order:

$$F-G-A-B-C-D-E$$

2: Apply the specified number of sharps or flats. F minor has four flats, so we take the first four from the "order of flats" rule:

$$F-G-\overset{(3)}{A}♭-\overset{(1)}{B}♭-C-\overset{(4)}{D}♭-\overset{(2)}{E}♭$$

Congratulations! You just saved $2,000 on your first semester of "Intro to Music Theory" in university. Back to the Parent Key approach.

As previously established, each mode prioritizes a different scale degree from the major scale. Let's take the key of C major and its associated modes:

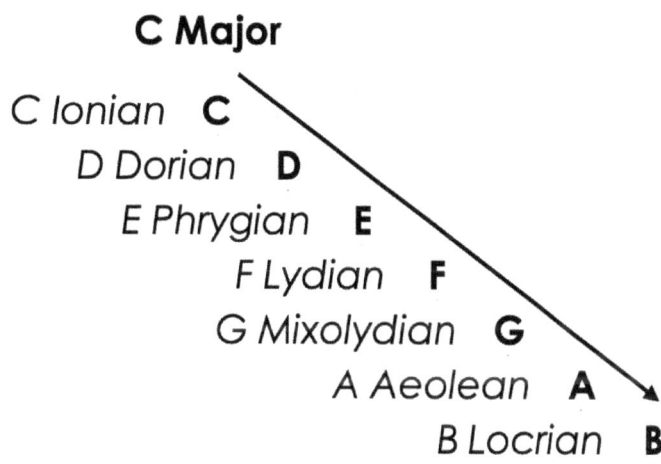

C Major

C Ionian **C**
D Dorian **D**
E Phrygian **E**
F Lydian **F**
G Mixolydian **G**
A Aeolean **A**
B Locrian **B**

Each of these modes use the exact same collection of notes from the C major scale, also known as the **Parent Key**. D Dorian uses the key of C major, meaning the parent key is *down* a major second from D to C. Similarly, E Phrygian is the third mode of C major, meaning its parent key is down a major third from E to C. The pattern continues for each of the modes in relation to the parent key as seen below:

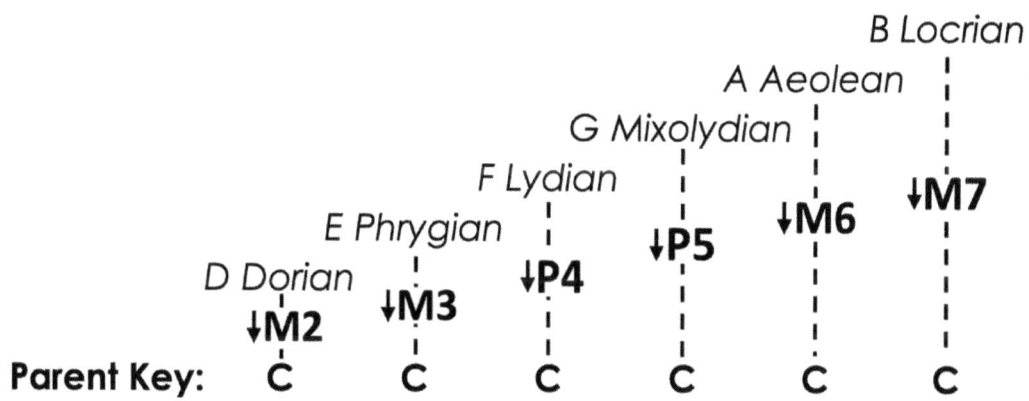

B Locrian
A Aeolean
G Mixolydian
F Lydian
E Phrygian
D Dorian
↓M2   ↓M3   ↓P4   ↓P5   ↓M6   ↓M7

Parent Key: C   C   C   C   C   C

These intervals are another "hard rule" that apply to all modes in theory and in practice. The specified mode tells you exactly what interval to go down and use the key signature from that parent key. The following diagram uses this hard rule to find the parent key (and therefore collection of notes) for each mode starting on C.

Mode	Interval	Parent Key	Notes
C Ionian	No Change	C Major(No Sharps/Flats)	C - D - E - F - G - A - B
C Dorian	↓ M2	B♭ Major(2 Flats)	C - D - E♭ - F - G - A - B♭
C Phrygian	↓ M3	A♭ Major(4 Flats)	C - D♭ - E♭ - F - G - A♭ - B♭
C Lydian	↓ P4	G Major(1 Sharp)	C - D - E - F♯ - G - A - B
C Mixolydian	↓ P5	F Major(1 Flat)	C - D - E - F - G - A - B♭
C Aeolean	↓ M6	E♭ Major(3 Flats)	C - D - E♭ - F - G - A♭ - B♭
C Locrian	↓ M7	D♭ Major(5 Flats)	C - D♭ - E♭ - F - G♭ - A♭ - B♭

Notice that the collection of notes for each mode is the exact same as the intervallic approach on page 42. It's the same soup, just reheated in a new way. Just like the intervallic approach, the parent key approach can be used for any mode starting on any pitch. It's a fast and easy way to "fill in the blanks" when struggling to find the right collection of notes.

Method 3: The Scale Degree Approach

I always hated when teachers would answer my questions with "because I'm your instructor and I said so", leaving no room for interpretation or opinion. There are very few things in the world of guitar that have only one answer, and this approach to modes is one of them.

Let's take the Lydian mode for example. If you play the Lydian mode starting on a different pitch 12 times over, *every single time* you are going to end up playing a major scale with a raised fourth scale degree. That's just the way Lydian is. That fourth scale degree may originally be flat and needs to be raised to a natural, or it may be natural and needs to be raised to a sharp, but no matter what that fourth scale degree will be raised compared to its regular position in the major scale. Because I said so.

C Lydian: C   D   E   F♯ G   A   B   C

Raised Fourth

As you may have guessed, this concept applies to all the modes. Each one has a specific number of modified scale degrees that can be memorized to instantly pull out a mode anywhere anytime. The following chart displays those modifications, do your best to memorize them for that instant shortcut.

Mode	Modified Scale Degree(s)
Ionian	No Change (Major Scale)
Dorian	♭3, ♭7
Phrygian	♭2, ♭3, ♭6, ♭7
Lydian	♯4
Mixolydian	♭7
Aeolean	♭3, ♭6, ♭7
Locrian	♭2, ♭3, ♭5, ♭6, ♭7

The good news is that if you know your major and minor scales, altering them to create modes is a breeze. Ionian? Play the major scale. Dorian? Play the natural minor scale, don't flat the 6. Phrygian? Play the natural minor scale and also flat the 2. Lydian? Major with a sharp 4. Mixolydian? Major with a flat 7. Aeolean? Play the natural minor scale. Locrian? Play the natural minor with a flat 2 and 5 (or Phrygian with a flat 5). The chart below applies these shortcuts to every mode starting on C:

Mode	Modified Scale Degree(s)	Starting On C
Ionian	No Change (Major Scale)	C - D - E - F - G - A - B
Dorian	♭3, ♭7	C - D - E♭ - F - G - A - B♭
Phrygian	♭2, ♭3, ♭6, ♭7	C - D♭ - E♭ - F - G - A♭ - B♭
Lydian	♯4	C - D - E - F♯ - G - A - B
Mixolydian	♭7	C - D - E - F - G - A - B♭
Aeolean	♭3, ♭6, ♭7	C - D - E♭ - F - G - A♭ - B♭
Locrian	♭2, ♭3, ♭5, ♭6, ♭7	C - D♭ - E♭ - F - G♭ - A♭ - B♭

The important distinction to make on the previous chart is that the shorthand for the modified scale degrees represent *raised* and *lowered* scale degrees, not literal sharps and flats. Take D major for example. This key has two sharps, F♯ and C♯:

$$D \quad E \quad F\sharp \quad G \quad A \quad B \quad C\sharp \quad D$$

Now let's say we want to play D Dorian, flat the 3 and the 7 right?

$$D \quad E \quad F\flat \quad G \quad A \quad B \quad C\flat \quad D$$

Wrong. If the scale degree is already sharp from the existing major scale, modifying it with a flat would lower it *twice* (F♯ - F natural – F♭). Remember that the shorthand means *lowering* the scale degree by one half-step, turning the F♯ and C♯ into F natural and C natural. You can always double check your work by looking for enharmonics (page 12). In the example above, F♭ and E natural are the same pitch, meaning they cannot be two different scale degrees. The same applies to C♭ and B natural in the example above.

Summary on the Three Approaches to Modes

The following example uses the three different approaches to modes to arrive at the same answer. Suppose we want to find the collection of notes for B Aeolian.

Method 1:

Aeolean is the sixth re-arrangement of the W-W-H-W-W-W-H sequence, giving us the interval sequence of W-H-W-W-H-W-W. Apply the sequence starting on B:

$$B \quad C\sharp \quad D \quad E \quad F\sharp \quad G \quad A \quad B$$
$$\vee \quad \vee \quad \vee \quad \vee \quad \vee \quad \vee \quad \vee$$
$$W \quad H \quad W \quad W \quad H \quad W \quad W$$

Method 2:

Aeolean is a major sixth above its major parent key, meaning we need to descend a major sixth from B to find our new key signature. A major sixth down from B gives us D natural, meaning we use the key signature of D major with two sharps:

B C♯ D E F♯ G A B

(2) above C♯, (1) above F♯

Method 3:

Aeolean has a flat 3, flat 6, and flat 7. Start with B major (5 sharps):

B C♯ D♯ E F♯ G♯ A♯ B

Now lower (not necessarily flat) the 3rd, 6th, and 7th:

B C♯ D E F♯ G A B

There is no right or wrong way to arrive at this collection of notes, all that matters is that you arrived at the right place and have some sort of consistent method for doing so. The beauty of modes is that everyone processes information differently, experiment with each of the methods and see what works best for you.

Modes on the Fretboard

No matter how you arrive at your modal conclusion, you're going to end up playing the same notes on the fretboard. The following diagrams are a good starting point to dabble in the emotions that each mode uniquely offers. Once again, each starting point will be on E for the sake of consistency.

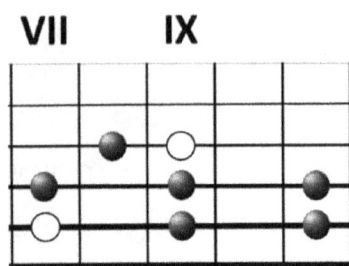

E Ionian

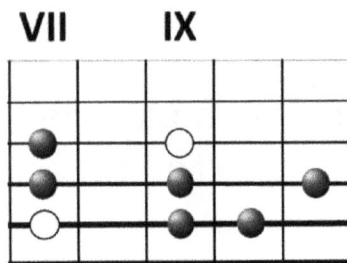

E Dorian

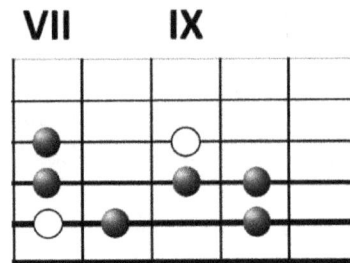

E Phrygian

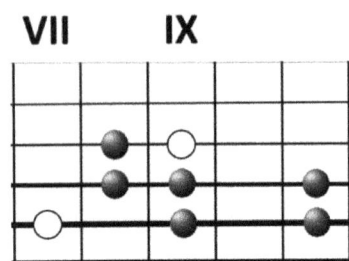

E Lydian

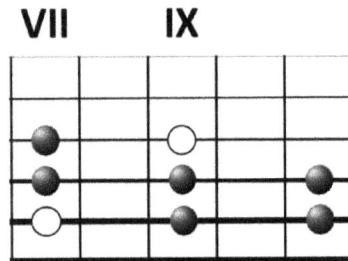

E Mixolydian

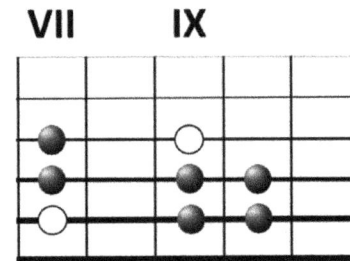

E Aeolean

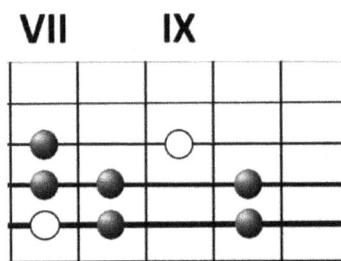

E Locrian

If modes have not blown your mind yet, go back and take a look at all the 3NPS patterns on page 37 and 38. Each of those forms are modes based around the note collection of form 1. For example, if the lowest open circle on the low E string of form 1 was placed on G (3rd fret), form 2 would be A Dorian, form 3 would be B Phrygian, and so on. You can also work the other way and say form 1 in 3rd position is G Ionian, form 2 in 3rd position is G Dorian, form 3 in 3rd position is G Phrygian, and so on. Modes appear to be quite complex in theory, but are quite simple in practice. As with all techniques, it's one thing to write out and put on the fretboard, but it's something else entirely to *feel*. While in practice, spend some time not only going up and down the shapes, but processing each unique emotion.

THE DIMINISHED LAYOUT

Diminished tonalities lay out quite nicely on the fretboard, and often have re-occurring patterns from position to position. The fully diminished quality naturally arises on the fretboard like so:

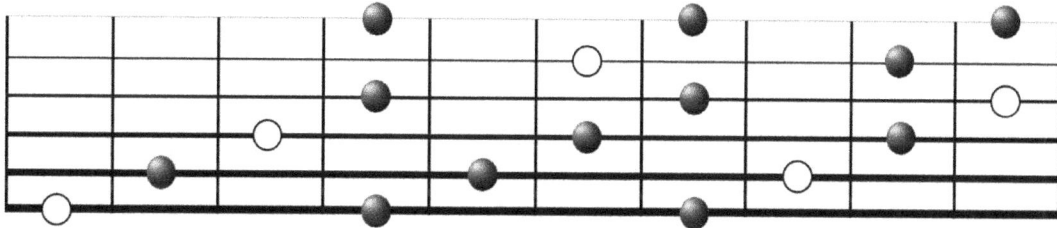

The most important intervallic relationship by far in a diminished tonality is the augmented fourth, also known as the tritone. Most guitarists see this interval as the classic "diagonally up one string, up one fret", which is abundant in the layout above. This layout can be broken down into smaller groups for individual voicings:

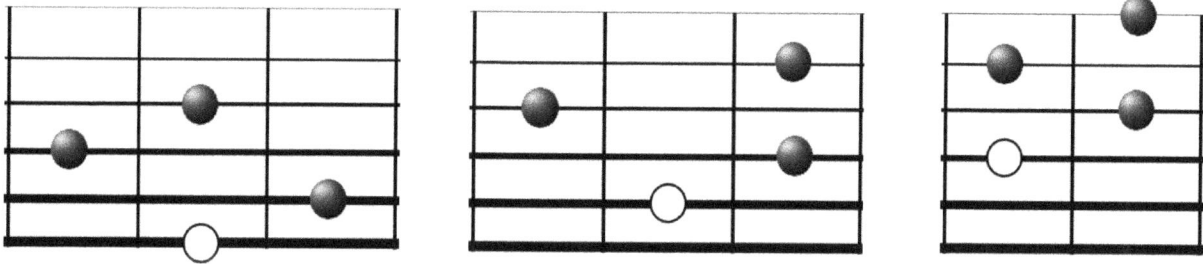

You'll probably notice that each of these patterns repeat themselves every three frets. In theory, a fully diminished chord is simply a bunch of minor thirds stacked on top of each other. Three frets on a guitar is the distance of a minor third, so essentially by moving the shape up or down three frets you're just re-ordering (inverting) the chord. Use this relationship to your advantage by sliding or shifting around to create interesting movements of tension. Similar to the CAGED system, the pattern is an endless loop that repeats itself until there are no more frets left to play.

THE CORPOREAL

APPLIED PHYSICAL TECHNIQUE

II

WARM-UPS

Warm-Ups can often be misconstrued as practice. While they are certainly part of a practice routine, warm-ups have a completely different objective. The goal of a **warm-up** session is to refamiliarize yourself with the fundamentals and mechanics of your specific instrument. Every guitar has its own unique feel derived from a combination of string action, scale length, string gauge, neck profile, and radius. Technical jargon aside, think of each guitar like a make and model of a car. The basic ideas and mechanics of driving are the same, but there can be a massive difference in feel and responsiveness between a minivan and a sports car. A successful warm-up session reactivates your muscle memory and physically synchronizes your fingers with what your brain is telling them to do. The following exercise uses one finger per fret and string, giving your brain the information it needs to re-engage its muscle memory:

This exercise can be repeated up or down any number of frets as desired until hand-eye coordination is synchronized. Speed will come with time, for now the important thing to focus on is accuracy.

Another common warm-up exercise is choosing a position and using one finger per fret on each string. Many guitarists refer to this one as "the spider", as seen below in fifth position:

Once again, the objective is to be as mechanically accurate as possible, using the tip of each finger to produce a clear, direct note with no fret buzz. Accuracy through dexterity is the only goal of these exercises, so try to play at a speed that enables you to individually express notes without cutting off or under-articulating them. Many guitarists find it all too easy to rush through these exercises to get to the "fun" sections of practice, missing the entire purpose of what a warm-up is. A warm-up session ends when your hand-eye coordination is in high-gear, not when you finish playing through a given exercise. For some people synchronization is found in five minutes, for others it may take twenty or thirty.

Left Hand Warm-Ups

The right hand will take care of articulation, it's the left hand's job to be on the correct string and fret when it's needed. An important skill to develop is the ability to "transfer" from one finger to another at *just* the right time to maintain clarity. There are 24 different combinations of left hand finger placements, each can be applied to the spider exercise to develop left hand fluidity:

1234	1243	1324	1342	1423	1432
2134	2143	2314	2341	2413	2431
3124	3142	3214	3241	3412	3421
4123	4132	4213	4231	4312	4321

The following is an example of the **2-3-1-4** variation applied to the spider in fifth position:

Right Hand Warm-Ups

The right hand is responsible for timing and articulation. Choosing a note to play is only half the battle; choosing *when* to play it is a whole other art form in itself. The muscles in your right arm and hand are a physical manifestation of your ability to execute or "feel", like gears moving in a clock. A successful right hand warm up re-calibrates these gears and ensures they are ready for use. One of the most effective exercises to start this process is a simple alternate picking pattern (more on this later) over a basic chord, like so:

This exercise can be repeated any number of times over any chord until a feeling of "calibration" is achieved. One way to develop a sense of calibration is to experiment with rhythm, as seen here:

Synchronization Warm-Ups

String-skipping exercises are a great way to refamiliarize yourself with the unique intimacies of your instrument. When performed correctly, they effectively synchronize your left and right hands while reminding them of small details like the distance between strings and the necessary amount of finger pressure to play notes without any buzz. Remember to GO SLOW while playing through the following exercise and focus on accuracy. The tortoise wins the race on this one:

The same exercise can also be performed in a descending run like so:

VARIATIONS ON THE MAJOR SCALE

Every developing guitarist has come across the major scale at some point on their musical journey. Whether the technical name is known or not, that infamous "Do Re Mi Fa Sol La Ti Do" (scale degrees 1 through 7 for those who have finished the scales chapter on page 8) has engrained itself into the very fibers of our subconscious. Since its creation in the 11th century (commonly credited to the Italian music theorist Guido of Arezzo) the scale has been taught linearly from bottom to top, like so:

Guitarists have since applied it to the fretboard in various ways, most commonly though Forms 1 and 5 of the 3NPS system (8th and 3rd positions for C Major):

Form 1

Form 5

These ideas are necessary to gain a basic understanding of fret relationships and keys, but if you're anything like me you have one fundamental problem with this approach. It isn't *music*. There is a monumental disconnect between the major scale in theory and in practice. What's the point of memorizing dictionaries of vocabulary if you can't use any of it in a sentence? Most theory and method books haven't figured it out yet, but we passed the 11th century some time ago. If I tap the little screen in my pocket in the right order, pizza shows up at my front door. What a time to be alive. It's time to start thinking of the major scale a little more creatively. The following variations should help get the creative juices flowing, the only limit here is your imagination.

Sequencing in Thirds

Breaking the major scale down into groups of three is a valuable method for disrupting an otherwise predictable phrase containing pulses of four. Resetting the sequence a beat early establishes a sense of controlled "stumbling", creating an unexpected level of interest for the listener. Once initiated, the groupings of three will realign with their original pulse after every twelve beats.

This expression reimagines that same linear momentum in a new way:

Groups of three can also be rhythmically stretched or condensed any number of ways to create a sense of contrast.

Groups of three (1-2-3) can also be harmonically rearranged (1-3-2):

Another interesting grouping could be (2-1-3):

Once again, the possibilities are endless here. A little creative input goes a long way in finding new expressions. As always, experiment and modify to taste, then incorporate your ideas into everyday use.

Drones and Common Tones

Another eccentric variation on the major scale is the use of drones or common tones to contrast a moving line against a stagnant anchor point. A **drone** is a reoccurring or sustained note that is generally assigned to a bass voice. Placing a drone in the bass provides a solid foundation to build intensity or experiment with color tones.

Thinking outside the box is always encouraged, why not put a drone in the top voice?

This idea can be expanded to create additional directionality. The listener is expecting the drone to remain stagnant, which means that breaking this expectation can result in some peculiar expressions. Shifting the drone evokes tension in the passage, sending the listener on somewhat of a journey to a resolution. Use the following expression as a framework for your own ideas on directionality and tension.

A **common tone** is a shared note between any neighboring chords in a progression and can be assigned to any voice. For example, the chords C major (C-E-G), F major (F-A-C), and A minor (A-C-E) all share the note C. the repetition of the note C will create an anchor point that offers stability over a changing progression.

This concept can be applied to any two (or more) chords that share the same note, so keep a lookout for opportunities to utilize it in your day-to-day practice.

LEGATO

The ability to execute a clean legato run is a fundamental skill that separates the novice from the developing guitarist. Unfortunately, there is some confusion around what legato exactly is. There are several definitions within the sizeable world of music depending on what area and archival time period one finds themselves in. For clarity's sake, we'll take a brief historical detour before applying the technique directly to the guitar.

Legato is an Italian term meaning "tied-together" when describing a sequence of notes. The term originally applied to singers as early as the 18th century, who were instructed to string together as many vowels as possible with minimal interruption from the sharp sounds of consonants. String instruments naturally emulate this concept by playing notes to their full duration, omitting any perceptible silence or space between note transitions. A well implemented legato line minimizes the initial "attack" of each given pitch, and connects the sustained pitches with minimal interruption. The modern guitar reconceptualizes legato in a variety of ways, most notably through the application of slides, bends, hammer-ons, and pull-offs (known as slurs to the classical guitarist). In summary, legato can be played on a guitar by sounding a series of notes without directly plucking them, thus evoking a feeling of fluidity or motion.

Sidenote: Legato is generally indicated by an overarching tie across a given passage of notes, like so:

While legato can be performed through a variety of techniques on the guitar, the most common are hammer-ons and pull-offs. A **Hammer-on** uses a left hand (playing hand) finger to swiftly press a string into a given fret, sounding a note without plucking it in the right hand (strumming hand). In theory it is possible to hammer-on a note anywhere on the fretboard out of thin air, but in practice many guitarists find that hammering-on the first note on a given string creates unwanted noise and overtones. Special preparation and care can be taken to avoid these additional sounds, but common practice dictates that the first note on a given string be plucked for a clean, crisp tone. Any subsequent notes on that same string can then be executed with a hammer-on, avoiding any undesired impurities. Hammer-ons are generally notated with an "H" in between any notes to be executed with the technique:

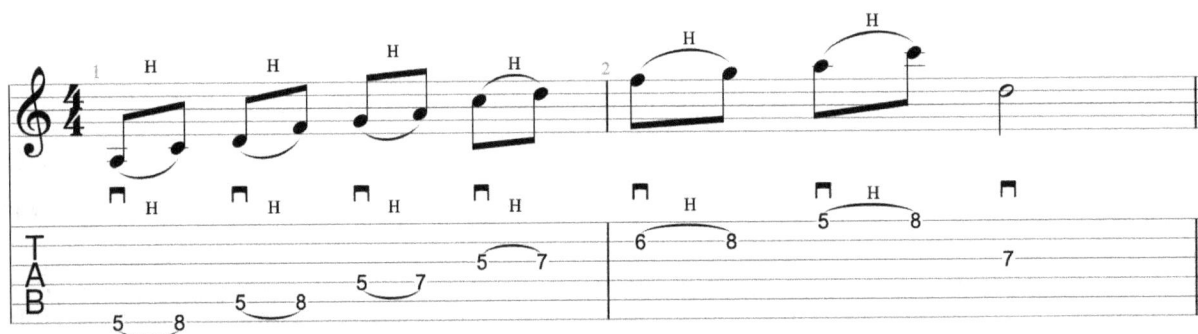

Where hammer-ons raise subsequent pitches, pull-offs are used to descend from previous notes. To perform a **pull-off**, simply use the left hand finger currently ringing a given note to "pluck" the string, in turn articulating a lower note on that same string (possibly the open string itself). Notice the use of the word "pluck" in that definition, as many beginning players misconstrue a pull-off as a *pull-away*. Removing the finger currently ringing a given note merely ends the duration of that note. In order to articulate a subsequent note, the finger responsible for ringing the first note needs to pluck the string in a downward motion towards the floor, much like a pick in the right hand.

Notes preceded by a "P" are to be played with a pull-off, like so:

A "legato run" commonly suggests a distance covered (ascending or descending) that employs legato throughout the passage:

Hammer-ons and pull-offs naturally coincide to produce a fluid legato sound:

Legato runs are a breeze when visualizing the 3NPS forms. The forms connect seamlessly, allowing continuity across longer distances. Use the following expression as a reference for developing your own connective strategies:

PICKING VARIATIONS

As a developing guitarist digs further and further down the rabbit hole of tone, a once obscure unknown moves to the forefront of considerations; *articulation*. It's what makes the voice of each guitarist identifiably unique, each note serving as an idiosyncratic experience picked up along the way. The following techniques can be used as general methods to emulate your favorite songs and solos, but remember that those tracks are recordings of an artist's personal experiences. They may attack a note with ferocity, or soothe a note out of tenderness and care. Make an effort to listen for and learn from these articulations, but remember that notes and experiences ultimately belong to each individual. Nobody can truly be duplicated.

Downpicking is an aggressive approach that forcefully articulates a collection of notes, leaving little in the way of nuance or reservation. Generally found in faster and heavier music, downpicking serves as a tool for delivering an extra "edge" to an otherwise passive phrase. As the name implies, each note in a downpicked passage is executed with a down stroke. This creates a rather inefficient wrist motion, as the pick needs to cycle back to the top of the string to re-articulate each and every down stroke. Use the technique with caution and care, as it is one of the leading causes of injuries like tennis elbow and carpal tunnel. When playing at full speed, try to relax as many muscles as possible instead of clenching and suffocating the pick. As always, start slow and build up speed. The tortoise wins the race on this one.

The most common articulation is alternate picking, as it has a wide variety of applications. Generally expressed in scales and melodic lines, the technique has planted itself under many guitarist's fingers as a go-to muscle memory routine. As you might have guessed, **alternate picking** simply alternates between down strokes and up strokes. Among the advantages of the technique are speed and consistency. A cyclical down-up-down-up revolution cuts the pick's travel time in half, allowing for much faster repetitions with a less perceivable difference in annunciation. Depending on the guitarist's specific need, it is usually best to choke up on the pick and leave less material exposed under the thumb, much like writing with a pencil for accuracy.

A slight variation on alternate picking, **tremolo picking** focuses on one or two notes and rapidly executes them in quick succession via alternate down and up strokes. This technique is great for the peak of melodic lines or solos, as it has somewhat of a flair for the dramatic. For additional spice, go back and refresh your memory on harmony in thirds (page 26). Implementing thirds in tremolo passages fills the space and creates additional interest. Along with downpicking, use caution when playing at full speed. Tensing up to play faster can have negative effects, so be sure to take breaks when feeling discomfort.

An additional variation or sub-classification of alternate picking, **cross picking** essentially alternate picks a grouping of notes to arpeggiate a given chord. This idea usually comes into play when mimicking bluegrass or folk instruments like banjos or mandolins.

```
  ┌3┐ ┌3┐ ┌3┐ ┌3┐    ┌3┐ ┌3┐ ┌3┐ ┌3┐
  ⊓ V ⊓ ⊓ V ⊓ ⊓ V ⊓ ⊓ V ⊓   ⊓ V ⊓ ⊓ V ⊓ ⊓ V ⊓ ⊓ V ⊓
T   1     1     1     1       3     3     3     5
A 0     0     0     0       0     0     0     0
B   2     2     2     2         3     3     3     5
```

Economy picking is a more advanced approach, as it requires the player to consider subsequent notes before choosing a picking direction and executing the current one. Localized to one string, the technique defaults to alternate picking. However, as notes shift across strings, the last note on the current string must be picked in the direction of the next string. This significantly reduces the pick's travel distance, eliminating the need to "over-correct" and move beyond a string only to come back and pick it in the opposite direction. Consider the following G major scale, executed with a standard alternate pattern:

```
  ⊓ V ⊓ V ⊓ V ⊓ V   ⊓ V ⊓ V ⊓ V ⊓
T                                   5   7   8
A               4   5   7       4   5   7
B 3   5   7   3   5   7       7
```

Notice the pick's inefficient travel motion when playing the B (7th fret E string) to the C (3rd fret A string). The pick has to travel beyond the A string only to come back and up stroke the C. A second case of inefficiency is seen between executing the E (7th fret A string) and the F# (4th fret D string). Due to its place in the alternate pattern, the E must be up stroked even though the following note lies on a string in the opposite direction. This forces the pick to pluck the string then travel immediately back across it to reach the next note in the sequence. Enter the economy picking technique:

Each note now considers the location of the next, optimizing for minimum distance travelled and maximum speed and efficiency.

Taking efficiency to the next level, **sweep picking** is a technique mastered by many virtuoso players. Depending on individual contexts, sweep picking is mainly used when arpeggiating chords across several strings in a row. With one note on each string, the pick travels in an immediate down-down-down or up-up-up motion, allowing the notes to be played as fast as the right hand can strum and the left hand can keep up. Arpeggio patterns lay out quite nicely when spread across the strings for sweeping:

Positions can also be connected with slides and pull-offs for a cleaner approach:

Hybrid picking maintains the use of a pick between the thumb and index finger, but also incorporates the middle and ring fingers to create chords or contrast bass and treble strings. This technique is also known as "chicken picking" and can be found all over country and folk styles. Standard notation uses down strokes for the picked note, "m" for notes plucked with the middle finger, and "a" for notes plucked with the ring finger. Notice the slight change in articulation between sharp picked notes and round plucked notes, as the use of finger tips to pluck the strings change the timbre in favor of a slightly warmer hue.

Some advanced country players like to combine pull-offs and slides while hybrid picking for runs with some extra "twang":

The final picking variation is that of abandoning the pick altogether for a traditional folk or classical feel. **Fingerstyle** is the use of the thumb (p), index (i), middle (m), and ring (a) fingers to pluck the strings with a warmer, intimate tone. To execute a given note, simply prepare your thumb or fingers over the necessary string(s) and close your hand in a swift, firm motion to make a fist. It may be worthwhile to experiment with nail shape and length for the right combination of warmth and attack.

It's best to prepare right hand fingerings in advance when playing fingerstyle material, as many developing players find themselves repeating fingers and stumbling through passages at full speed. While there is no perfect system for knowing which right hand finger to use, in general it's considered poor technique to immediately re-use the same finger twice (especially three times) in a row. The analogy here would be like typing on a keyboard with your two index fingers, when proper technique calls for all fingers to be evenly spaced across the keys, each with their own designated responsibilities. When in doubt with fingerstyle, use a pattern that most naturally allows the hand to close itself and make a fist from the outer pinky to the inner index finger. The fingers can then reset and prepare for their next position and time to "close". Every once in a while, you may come across a player who "flicks" the strings in an outward motion. If it works for their particular situation then great, but in general it's best to avoid the habit as its seen as particularly poor technique. While there's technically no such thing as "wrong" in the world of art and music, just know that these types of moves are highly frowned upon in the context of higher education.

ORNAMENTS

Just like the wide scope of the English language, music has its own localized dialects with individual quirks. Vocabulary holds the same meaning, but may be emphasized in a different manner. Think of these next techniques as linguistic accents that solidify your personal identity. Process and experiment with each of them to find a voice of your own.

One of the most common ornaments, bends are a great way to approach a given note with added directionality or interest. **Bending** uses fingers in the left hand to displace the string, increasing the string's tension and raising the pitch to a given note. Give extra attention to the accuracy of the bent note, as it is all too easy to under or over bend yourself out of tune. An in-tune bend is the mark of a developed guitarist, so be sure to spend some time listening for pitch and memorizing how much pressure is needed to displace each string. Notes on the lower strings and frets will require more pressure to bend to pitch, while notes on the higher strings and frets have more "give" and require less energy to displace. Keep in mind that staying within a given key requires some notes to be bent up a whole step (notated as "full"), while others only need to be bent up a half step (notated as ½). While practicing bend accuracy, it's always a good idea to give yourself a reference pitch. The following example uses notes on the B string as a pitch guide for notes on the G string to bend to:

As a general rule, strings are bent towards the center of the fretboard. This means that the High E, B, and G strings are pushed up towards the ceiling, while the Low E, A, and D strings are pulled down towards the floor. If you're having trouble mustering enough strength in a single finger to execute a specific bend, remember that you can support that finger with others behind it. For example, your first and second fingers can be used to support your third finger to bend a string up to pitch.

Pre-bends are a crafty technique to play with the listeners expectations. A **Pre-bend** is performed by pre-emptively bending a string to pitch, THEN plucking the note and releasing the string down to its regular tension. This one is easier said than done, as it requires the pre-bent string to be held in perfect tension before hearing a sound. The listener hears a normally fretted tone, but the deception comes when the pitch bends down into a new note. This is particularly effective on guitars without a tremolo bridge (AKA whammy bar), as one is usually needed to achieve the same sound. Pre-bends are notated with a vertical up-arrow followed by a descending down-arrow until the string's tension has been released:

Once again, using a reference tone on another string is a great way to develop your ear for staying in tune and your muscle memory for the correct finger strength required to bend strings to pitch. As usual, a word of warning when applying bends to your vocabulary. A few targeted expressions here and there are great, but too many in a row cause wishy-washy phrases that can be quite hard to follow.

Slides are another ornament that embellish one's vocabulary and overall expression. A rather self-explanatory technique, **slides** use a left hand finger to transfer from one note to another on the same string. The trick is to keep pressure while moving fast enough to prevent "dragging" across individual frets, but slow enough to hear the effect. How you choose to start and stop a slide will also affect your sound, so be sure to listen for inflection and accents.

Some advanced players will slide into a note from seemingly thin air, maintaining the sound of a slide while omitting the starting note. In reality a slide has to start *somewhere*, but that starting note doesn't necessarily need attention drawn to it. This introduces the idea of a **grace note**, a pre-emptive starting pitch that has no rhythmic value. Grace notes are usually a half or whole step away from the target note, and serve only as a starting location for your finger before immediately sliding into the desired fret. Grace notes are indicated by a smaller note directly to the left of the target note, and are executed *just* before the target note lands on its intended beat.

If you've ever heard a shredding guitar solo from the 80's, you may already be familiar with the idea of tapping. While there are a variety of ways to go about it, **tapping** uses a right hand finger (or pick) to hammer-on and pull-off a note on the fretboard that would otherwise be unavailable to the left hand. In theory, any note can be tapped using the right hand, although taking the time to reposition and place it on the fretboard can create inefficiencies. For this reason, most guitarists will tap a sequence of notes, keeping the right hand stable in one location and avoiding the back-and-forth motion between plucking and tapping. For example, consider the following E minor arpeggio:

Moving vertically up the strings keeps the left hand in one position, but creates stumbling when repeated and severely limits speed. Now what would happen if the left hand could stretch beyond its physical ability? The introduction of the right hand on the fretboard (notated by a "T" for Tap) re-imagines the string as a horizontal keyboard, releasing the left hand from its physical restrictions:

Remember that just like a left hand pull-off, the tapped note will need to be plucked (not just removed) to articulate the subsequent note.

A considerably more subtle ornament, vibrato provides a sophistication to an otherwise impersonal tone. Adding **vibrato** to a note gently pulls it in and out of tune, creating a slight warble that gives the note (and therefore the guitarist) a distinct identity. Of all the guitarists in the world, no one will warble a note at quite the same speed or with the same intensity. It is a skill that takes a great amount of discipline to apply correctly and with taste, so really take some extra time to listen for the nuance between different players. A developed guitarist employs the technique to introduce dimension with surgical precision, an overlooked idea that remains unobtrusive and is really only noticed when absent. The electric guitar is the only string instrument that manipulates vibrato by bending vertically (like a normal half or whole step bend), whereas acoustic (especially nylon/classical) guitars traditionally add vibrato by horizontally moving the left hand back and forth in a rocking motion. In either case, vibrato is notated by a wavy line across the duration of the note. The larger the wave, the wider and more intense the vibrato:

If an expression calls for an intense enough vibrato, one might consider using a trill instead. Notated by "tr", a **trill** rapidly alternates between two notes, usually a half step apart:

Another somewhat subtle technique is the **palm-mute**, where the edge of the right hand palm slightly rolls past its resting point on the bridge to make contact with the string(s). The more contact the palm makes with the end of the string, the more muted that string becomes, removing more and more of a note's initial attack. Palm muting is a valuable method for creating a background and foreground in a passage, as it draws the listener's attention to intended accents. Palm muted notes are expressed with a "P.M." followed by a dotted line that extends across any additional notes to be muted.

Accented notes can also be brought to the foreground by utilizing a rake. A **rake** scrapes across several muted lower strings before digging into a note on a higher string. The muted scraping sound creates a texture that evokes a sense of aggression, as the movement requires a swift and firm right-hand strike through the strings. Muted lower strings can either be palm-muted with the right hand, or deadened by gently placing a left hand finger across the strings. When using the left hand to mute, remember not to place fingers directly in line on top of the frets, as this may cause unintentional harmonics to sound. Rakes are notated by the word "rake", with muted "X" grace notes leading up to the intended accented note:

The following ornaments require somewhat of a scientific preamble to understand exactly how a string can be manipulated into producing a harmonic. A **harmonic** is simply a higher frequency pitch in relation to a lower fundamental tone. These higher frequencies have very specific fractional relationships to distances on a given string. Think of an open string like a jump rope that oscillates between two points on either end:

Placing a harmonic at the exact half-way point of that distance doubles the frequency of the oscillation, creating a harmonic one octave above the fundamental note of the open string. By design, that location is directly above the 12th fret on all guitars. Gently place a left hand finger directly above the 12th fret on any string to "cut" the string in half and produce an octave harmonic:

12th Fret

Splitting the open string's distance in half *again* creates a harmonic two octaves above the fundamental note of the open string. To split the distance in fourths, gently hover a left hand finger above the 5th fret:

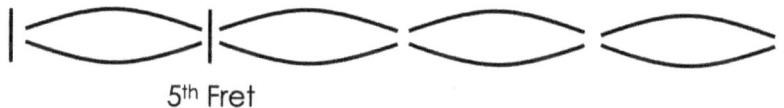

5th Fret

Keep in mind that these oscillations are perfectly symmetrical from the center of the string outwards. For example, playing a harmonic on the 24th fret will produce the same 2-octave harmonic as the 5th fret, as the open string is still technically being split into fourths:

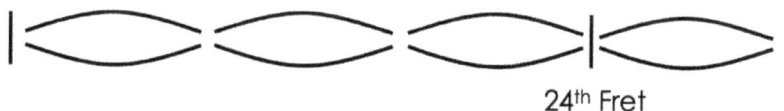

24th Fret

Try your hand at experimenting with different fractional relationships on different frets. You may notice that the 7th fret (and therefore the 19th) splits the string in thirds creating a perfect fifth above the fundamental, or that the 4th fret (and therefore the 9th, 16th, and theoretically 28th) splits the string in fifths creating a major third above the fundamental. A foundational understanding of harmonic relationships across the six strings will greatly enhance your vocabulary and note choice, so study up!

Fractional relationships that present themselves across the open strings are known as **natural harmonics**, and limit note choice to specific intervals in relation to the tuning of the open strings E, A, D, G, and B. Most notes can be found through one of these relationships, but some remain in an unwanted octave or are simply an impractical fraction that does not physically resonate on a string. For example, E natural can be found right on the 12th fret of the E string, and F# can be found on the 7th fret of the B string (perfect fifth above B), but finding an F natural as a natural harmonic is nearly impossible.

An **artificial harmonic** preserves the fractional-distance relationship of an open string, but moves it to a specific fret in order to sound an otherwise unreachable chromatic pitch. The important concept to take away is that the exact distance of a natural harmonic is preserved, that distance has just been relocated to a new starting point.

For example, the distance between the open high E string and the 12th fret is the exact same as the distance between the 1st and 13th frets. That octave harmonic has simply moved its fundamental pitch to the F natural on the 1st fret. To execute the artificial harmonic, use your left hand to fret the F natural on the 1st fret of the high E string while simultaneously hovering your right hand's pointer finger over the 13th fret and plucking the string with your right hand's middle or ring finger. Poof! F natural.

An additional variation to the natural harmonic is the pinch harmonic, which requires a specific plucking technique. A **pinch harmonic** exposes the right hand's thumb to make contact on the string while plucking to achieve a sharp squeal, generally heard with high gain or distortion. Pinch harmonics are an advanced technique that require a delicate balance of material between the pick and exposed thumb, and must be plucked at a specific fractional distance along the string. For example, fretting the E on the 9th fret of the G string while pinching at the 28th fret (just above the neck pickup on most electric guitars) will preserve a string distance of 1/3, sounding a B natural (octave plus a perfect fifth):

Once again, experiment with these relationships then add to taste.

FRETBOARD INTUITION

A truly developed guitarist transcends their title and identifies as a *musician*; an artist that utilizes the guitar as a medium of expression for what they are trying to say. The guitar is only the tool, the music that flows through it is an extension of the person playing it. Fretboard intuition is the ability to cut through the mental gymnastics and physical complexities of the guitar to allow an expression to flow straight from the mind of the musician to the ear of the listener. There are no physical or mental obstacles interrupting the musical idea. These intuitions present themselves in different ways, and are worth exploring on your journey to musical development.

The guitar is an instrument like no other in its ability to replicate the character and mannerisms of almost any other instrument. Other instruments are able to play notes simultaneously (polyphonic instruments), rhythmically (percussive instruments), or even microtonally (string instruments), but no other instrument possesses all three qualities. They are all somehow limited by range, pitch, duration, monophony, dynamic, articulation, or speed. Therein lies the beauty and the curse of the most complex instrument in history; *everything is possible*. So, what does a guitarist think about when playing? One approach is not to think like a guitarist at all:

The guitar finds itself at a somewhat transitional time in history. Not popularized until the 19th century, the instrument emerged at a time where symphony orchestras reigned at the pinnacle of forward-thinking music. Guitars were seen as a folk instrument to be played in intimate settings with little contribution to musical progress. This reputation continued well into the 20th century, until songwriters gave the instrument its own identity. If the entire course of music history was represented by an hour, the guitar has really only had its identity for the last minute and a half.

Due to the instrument's relative lack of historical credibility, many consider the guitar to be a platform for reproducing the ideas of more established instruments.

Much like the musical role of a piano, the guitar has the ability to provide a solid foundation of chord accompaniment. Linear in nature, the piano prefers to invert chords and remain stationary rather than preserve chord voicings (root-3rd-5th) and jump from location to location. Consider the following progression:

$$E\ minor \rightarrow B\ minor \rightarrow D\ Major \rightarrow A\ Major \rightarrow$$
$$C\ Major \rightarrow G\ Major \rightarrow B7$$

A piano would invert the chords required to maintain position, hold notes in common, and voice-lead notes to the next closest voicing solution:

Applied to the guitar, this progression and accompaniment pattern really only leave the guitarist with one logical voicing solution. Of all the positions to play an E minor chord, take a few minutes to try and find the most efficient starting point for the progression:

The trick to finding the most logical fretboard location in this case is to think like a piano player. Pianos prioritize triads, which are most efficiently played on the top (thin) strings of a guitar. The intervallic relationships between the G, B, and E strings provide the most opportunities to barre fingers across frets, maintain positions (one finger per fret), and cluster triads together without awkward stretches or shifts:

Playing the same progression on the lower (thicker) strings would result in fewer common fingers, more awkward stretches, poor note separation, and less efficient voice leading:

Keeping these nuances in mind, the most intuitive position to start the original E minor progression on the previous page would be seventh position, playing the E minor chord in "A" form of the CAGED system. Notice that the third finger is used as a **guide finger**, where it provides stability by staying on the same string (in this case the D string) while moving between chords. There are also several opportunities to barre the first finger across multiple strings, optimizing for less finger movement and condensed triad voicings. While a case can be made for starting the progression in 12th position, objectively speaking 7th position is the most physically efficient and provides the best voice-leading:

When a guitarist's job is to provide chord accompaniment, it's generally a good idea to think like a piano player. Prioritize triads, invert chords as necessary to optimize voice-leading, and think structurally to provide a foundational harmony. Fretboard intuitions will begin to present themselves when thinking about physical efficiencies like guide fingers, barre chords, CAGED movements, and finger placements.

When a guitarist's job is to provide the melody, an entirely new mindset should be adopted. While the notes of a melody certainly contribute to the overall chord harmony, they are a more significant contributor to the music's individual identity. Melody notes require intentional forethought to provide direction, without them a progression would move aimlessly with no real substance or value. Melodies are often assigned to prominent solo or monophonic instruments like violins, flutes, trumpets, and especially singers. When designing or playing through a melody, it's always beneficial to consider the physical characteristics of these instruments and how they would treat a melodic line.

Monophonic instruments like flutes, trumpets, and singers generally have a smaller range, which limits note movements and discourages large intervallic leaps. To guitarists and pianists, physically playing notes two or more octaves apart is as easy as pressing down a finger. Instruments that draw their notes from the human body (wind, brass, and vocals) follow a completely different set of mannerisms. They need to sound a note in their head then execute it, essentially pulling it out of thin air without being sharp or flat. To aid them in such a difficult task, many of these instrumentalists develop a strong sense of relative pitch. Once a given note is played, it serves as a reference point for pitches in close proximity, making them much easier to play in tune. Larger intervallic leaps begin to lose their sense of relativity, making them harder and harder to execute. Melody notes in a given range become targeted and precise, and are much easier to perform with feel and intent. The question for guitarists is where on the fretboard would a singer play?

Generally speaking, the middle of the fretboard is the most advantageous place to be when playing a melody. Somewhere between the seventh to ninth positions offer the most tonal and physical flexibility. Expressions played in lower positions often run into perceivable stumbles, as descending lines run out of frets and are forced to shift on to lower strings.

First position has limited physical maneuverability and few opportunities to add expressions that make the guitar "sing". The higher the position, the more flexible a string becomes, making it easier to embellish with vibrato. Notes played on lower frets also sound thinner and colder in comparison to notes played in higher positions:

Don't forget to think about the physical intimacies of the guitar when exploring fretboard intuition. When possible, keeping notes connected on the same string will maintain continuity and prevent unwanted changes in tone. A melody expressed well on the fretboard minimizes awkward shifts, but ultimately prioritizes the sound and feel of the expression. Don't be afraid to move outside a position's box, let your ear be the guiding factor as opposed to your fingers. Keeping these ideas in mind, the center of the fretboard offers warmer tone with more finger placement solutions and opportunities to enhance with ornaments. Ornaments fill an expression with character, and give the notes a voice. Remember to think like a singer, and sooner or later your guitar will start to sing.

THE EXPERIENTIAL

APPLIED TEMPORAL TECHNIQUE

III

TENSION AND RELEASE

The entirety of Western music can be summarized by these two ideas. Yin and yang, light and dark, ebb and flow, balance and instability. The main idea to take away is that these things happen across time. Just as the painter paints with brushes and canvas, the musician paints with notes and time. A truly developed guitarist creates an experience that a listener can connect to, with tension and release as their primary tools of the trade.

Tension is the anticipation a listener feels, creating a need for resolution. This anticipation can be developed a number of different ways:

One of the most common ways to synthesize a feeling of anticipation is through reiteration. Repeating a rhythmic idea elongates the duration of a listener's experience, thus building anticipation:

```
                3     3     3     3                    2
4/4  (repeated triplet chords)                        #8
                                                       o
                                                       o
T  4   4   4   4   4   4   4   4   4   4   4   4        6
A  5   5   5   5   5   5   5   5   5   5   5   5        7
B  5   5   5   5   5   5   5   5   5   5   5   5        7
   3   3   3   3   3   3   3   3   3   3   3   3        5
```

```
        3   3   3   3           3   3   3   3            3
4/4                           2                          #8
                                                         o
                                                         o
T  4 4 4 4 4 4 4 4 4 4 4 4   4 4 4 4 4 4 4 4 4 4 4 4     6
A  5 5 5 5 5 5 5 5 5 5 5 5   5 5 5 5 5 5 5 5 5 5 5 5     7
B  5 5 5 5 5 5 5 5 5 5 5 5   5 5 5 5 5 5 5 5 5 5 5 5     7
   3 3 3 3 3 3 3 3 3 3 3 3   3 3 3 3 3 3 3 3 3 3 3 3     5
```

Rhythmic ideas can also be contracted or sped up to increase the sense of intensity. Doubling a note's rhythmic value or increasing rhythmic frequency through triplets are great ways to build suspense:

Notice that throughout the examples above, the rhythm gets faster, but the *tempo* remains constant. For optimal results, try practicing these rhythmic variations with a metronome, as unintentional fluctuations in tempo are a sign you need more practice.

With that in mind, *intentional* changes in tempo will also build anticipation. Progressively speeding up an expression evokes a feeling of anxiety, like a heart beating faster and faster. If you're playing with a group, be sure to spend some extra time synchronizing these tempo changes. Having different members playing at different tempos is the fastest way to show a lack of preparation and cohesion. When in doubt, follow the drummer. To maximize the effect of the tempo change, it's important to land and follow through on the new tempo without rushing. If the release is rushed, the listener may not understand the intent of the change, and will begin to lose their connection to the music.

Another method for developing anticipation is the use of dynamics. Just like speaking, changes in volume can be used to express the musician's intimacy or frustration. Increasing a passage's volume builds intensity, while decreasing it naturally has the opposite effect. Use the chart below as a reference for volume relativity:

Symbol	Dynamic	Volume
pp	Pianissimo	Very Soft
mp	Mezzo-Piano	Medium Soft
mf	Mezzo-Forte	Medium Loud
f	Forte	Loud
ff	Fortissimo	Very Loud

Gradual changes in volume are notated by hairpins, where expanding hairpins represent a volume increase and contracting hairpins represent a volume decrease. These gradual volume adjustments are called **crescendos** and **decrescendos**, respectively.

Listeners also feel anticipation through motion. When an expression begins to move or move faster, the listener loses their foundation and is taken into an area of uncertainty. To be in motion is to move in a given direction, and one of the best ways to imply direction is to use ascending (or descending) stepwise motion, like so:

Unstable chromatic notes also evoke a feeling of anticipation, as chromaticism brings dissonance, and dissonance demands resolution. The key to embellishing with chromaticism is to use it as a technique to arrive at a targeted note. **Target notes** are important "identity" notes that suggest a specific chord or direction. Targeting the 3rd of a chord is generally most effective:

Release, or resolution, is the natural consequence of tension. Material held in anticipation dissipates, and the listener re-establishes their sense of stability. Rhythms slow down, dynamics are finalized, and chromaticism reaches its destination. Release will often write itself, the only decision for the player to make is how effective they want that release to be.

Many ideas are finalized by a musical punctuation mark known as a **cadence**. Cadences are the final resolution a listener experiences at the end of a phrase, and vary in strength and finality.

A **perfect authentic cadence** is known to be the strongest and most final, like a period at the end of a sentence. In order for a cadence to be a perfect authentic, the final chord must land in root position, with the tonic as the highest note in the chord:

```
B V
    5       7       8
    6       8       8
    5       7       9
    7       5       10
    8               10
                    8
```

An **imperfect authentic cadence** still finalizes a musical thought, but is slightly weaker as the resolution has less effective voice-leading. An imperfect authentic cadence is characterized by the final chord, where a note other than the tonic is the highest note in the chord, and/or the chord is inverted, placing a note other than the tonic in the bass:

```
B V         B III       B V
    5           3           8
    6           3           5
    7           4           5
    7           5           7
    5           5
                3
```

Similar to a comma or semicolon in English, the **half cadence** offers a resting point in a musical idea, but suggests there is more to come. That point generally rests on a dominant chord, more on those in the next section.

(Half Cadence)

As the name implies, a **rhythmic cadence** resolves the listener's feeling of anticipation by modifying the rhythm of an expression. Note values expand, bringing the musical idea to a close. Notice this example can be experienced just by tapping the rhythm alone:

Once a listener experiences tension, they naturally expect resolution. To play with these expectations, musicians can resolve to different tonal areas. Misdirecting the listener and resolving to a six chord (see next section) is known as a **deceptive cadence**:

CHORD FUNCTION

Some of the greatest composers, songwriters, and musicians in history have one thing in common: a complete understanding of the experiential system known as chord function. When writing, **chord function** refers to the tonal hierarchy of a key's diatonic chords and their relationship to the tonic. When a famous musician says "that song wrote itself", what they're really saying is that they followed a guiding method of harmonic organization. Each chord leads to the next in a seamless expression, travelling through phases of stability and instability. In order to understand the guiding system of chord function, it's important to be familiar with a key's diatonic chords, as each offer a slightly different color and implication. Each key from the circle of fifths (page 43) has seven scale degrees. Building a triad off each scale degree results in a key's seven diatonic chords, named and notated in roman numerals as follows:

I	ii	iii	IV	V	vi	vii°	I
Tonic	Super Tonic	Mediant	Sub Dominant	Dominant	Sub Mediant	Leading Tone	Tonic

Notice that roman numerals for major triads are uppercase, whereas numerals for minor triads are lowercase. The only diminished chord naturally occurs on the triad build off the seventh scale degree, notated by a lowercase numeral followed by the degree symbol. These chord qualities remain constant for any and all major keys, so the important takeaway here is to focus on chord movements and relationships, not necessarily the literal chord being played. In other words, don't worry about playing a G Major and C Major chord, focus on the dominant to tonic relationship.

The idea of chord function is that each chord plays a role in the path a progression takes from start to finish. Every chord lies somewhere on the spectrum of stability. More stable chords provide a resting point, as they produce less of a need to move on to another chord. Less stable chords heighten a sense of tension (anticipation), and require the progression to move faster towards a resolution. These ideas can be grouped into categories of functions, each with a varying sense of stability:

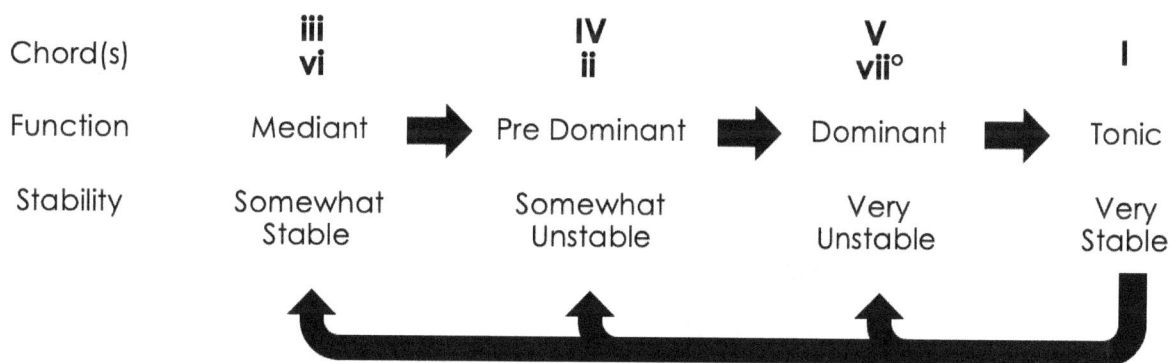

Chord(s)	iii vi	IV ii	V vii°	I
Function	Mediant ➡	Pre Dominant ➡	Dominant ➡	Tonic
Stability	Somewhat Stable	Somewhat Unstable	Very Unstable	Very Stable

Chords can be (and often are) substituted and expectations can be manipulated, but the overwhelming majority of progressive music follows some version of the narrative above. A progression starts on the tonic to establish a sense of home-base, then shifts to a mediant function to begin a movement. The movement progresses to a pre dominant function, where instability develops and evolves into the pinnacle of tension at the dominant function. Tensions resolve, and the listener re-establishes their sense of home-base back at the tonic. Notice that the tonic function in the diagram above has arrows to all the other functions, indicating that the tonic can essentially insert itself at any given point in the cycle, as all roads eventually lead back to itself pending one exception. As we discovered in the section on release, dominant chords can sometimes deceptively resolve, usually to a vi chord with a mediant function. Take some time to experiment with the expectations brought about by the narrative above, then try to apply them to some of your favorite songs to see what happens!

As you play through and experiment with various chord relationships, you may find that certain movements are more effective than others. Some wander aimlessly, while others are exceedingly directional and to the point. The most effective chord movement by far is to descend a perfect fifth, where the listener senses a strong and intentional pull into the next chord. From the tonic, chords descend in perfect fifths in an endless loop, commonly known as circle progression:

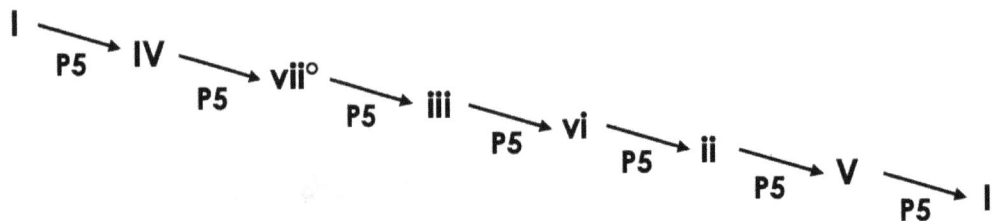

Playing through the entire circle progression can be somewhat of a prolonged journey, and is definitely the scenic route to get back to the tonic. The following diagram omits different variations of chords from the circle progression for a more direct approach. Be sure to think about the function of each chord and its implication on the next one in the progressions below:

I	IV	vii°	iii	vi	ii	V	I	Condensed Progression
I	--					V	I	I – V – I
I	-------------------------------------				ii	V	I	I – ii – V – I
I	IV	------------------------------				V	I	I – IV – V – I
I	--------------------			vi	ii	V	I	I – vi – ii – V – I

These are some of the most common progressions in music, and tap into a fundamental understanding that the listener may not be able to name, but is definitely able to feel. The vast majority of expressions that feel "classically correct" follow this tonal hierarchy. Thorough analysis of chord function will result in a quality understanding of the underlying identity of the music itself, a rich connection that developed guitarists draw from every day.

Understanding chord function is an invaluable skill, but unfortunately is not one that is always applicable. Not all music is written to be a dynamic journey full of progressive twists and turns, sometimes it's alright to just sit back and vibe. The experience doesn't necessarily have to be stagnant, but it doesn't need to be complex either. Sometimes a musician with a straightforward idea shared in the right way is just as impactful as an elaborate and powerful progression played by a full symphony orchestra. One of the simplest yet most effective musical expressions is the twelve bar blues. Love it or hate it, every developed guitarist should be familiar with the vocabulary and structure of a standard twelve bar blues, as it is a primary means of communication among many guitarists. The entire form only uses the three primary chords from a given major key:

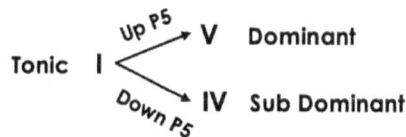

Just like progressive music, the tonic represents home, the sub dominant function represents a journey away from home, and the dominant function represents anticipation and an impending return back to home. These three functions are arranged over a standard form of twelve bars:

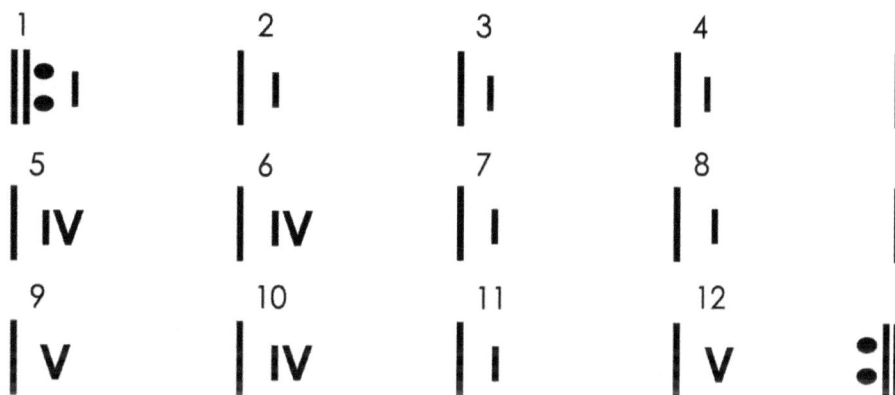

The twelve bar blues is an exceedingly valuable resource to draw from, as plenty of "non-progressive" music takes inspiration from the simplicity and freedom of movement.

PHRASING

Phrasing is at the core of what makes a developed guitarist. The ability to synthesize an idea then communicate it in such a way that the listener can connect to is practically the entire point of the guitar and music in general. Ever have one of those conversations that goes "hey, have you heard that song that goes nah nah nah nah nah?" "no, you're thinking of nuNAH nana nana"? That's phrasing. Tone, inflection, rhythm, note choice, dynamics, tempo, and articulation each play a part in the creation of every musical thought. **Phrasing** is the way a musician shapes the notes of a passage to create an expression, much like a person shapes words to form a sentence. Depending on a song's complexity and length, phrases are usually organized by one of the following:

- Four bar phrases are short and to the point. They are designed to hook in the listener and connect to them with a minimal barrier to entry. Many pop and rock songs intentionally use four bar phrasing.

- Eight bar phrases are a standard length, and generally offer a contrast between main and supporting ideas. Eight bar phrases are long enough to deliver substance, but short enough to understand on the first listen.

- Sixteen bar phrases allow the main and supporting ideas to expand, developing the vocabulary through evolutions of rhythms and note sequences. Sixteen bar phrases will usually take a couple extra listen-throughs to understand and latch on to.

- Thirty-two bar phrases are a full narrative, where melodic expressions have developed to their highest potential and value. These phrases require active listening to digest and interpret.

For a good exercise, count out the next few songs you listen to and measure where the singer (or melody) come to a natural resting point.

One of the most important skills to employ when creating a phrase is the use of motivic development. A **motive** is a small theme or group of notes that is legitimized through repetition. A few notes here and there are practically meaningless, but an intentionally repeated motive establishes a pattern that the listener can more easily latch on to. Consider the following motive:

In order to expand and develop the idea, it's important to know *what* we're developing. Motives consist of two basic concepts: rhythm, and melodic note choice. The rhythm of this idea is simple and easy to identify:

The note choice is also fairly straightforward, outlining the root, third, and fifth of an A Minor chord (A-C-E). Notice the ascending motion from the low A to high E. While repeating the rhythm, we can take advantage of this directionality to expand and target the next chord:

As the ascending motion reaches its peak, it targets the 3rd of D minor (F natural), then rests back on the new chord's root. Target notes are an essential strategy for creating an intentional and directional phrase. Take advantage of the ornaments section on page 72 to hit target notes in unique ways, like slides, bends, pre-bends, and harmonics. Often times less is more when phrasing. Arrive at the right note at *just* the right time and people will think you're a genius.

Notice the rhythmic space at the end of each idea, leaving a buffer to let the listener know that one idea has come to an end, and another is beginning. Leaving space at the end of the phrase also lets it breathe, just like a singer would naturally pause and take a breath before moving on. The next four bars (five through eight) are a useful "connecting" phrase that legitimize the original statement through repetition, but also build intensity to deliver the listener into the next eight measures. Directly repeating an idea doesn't do much for development, so consider keeping the interest through variation:

One of the best ways to build intensity is through sequences, which repeat a note pattern to transition into a new arrival, usually an octave or two from the starting point. Check out the variations on the major scale section on page 57 for a refresher on sequential ideas. Measures seven and eight could be re-written like so:

As time goes on, the listener becomes accustomed to the language and feel of the expression. The further into the phrases, the more liberties can be taken. Use the following expression as a guide to generate your own thoughts on phrasing and melodic development. Remember that the previous chapters are cumulative up to this moment, drawing from them will give you all the tools you need to enrich your expressions to their full potential.

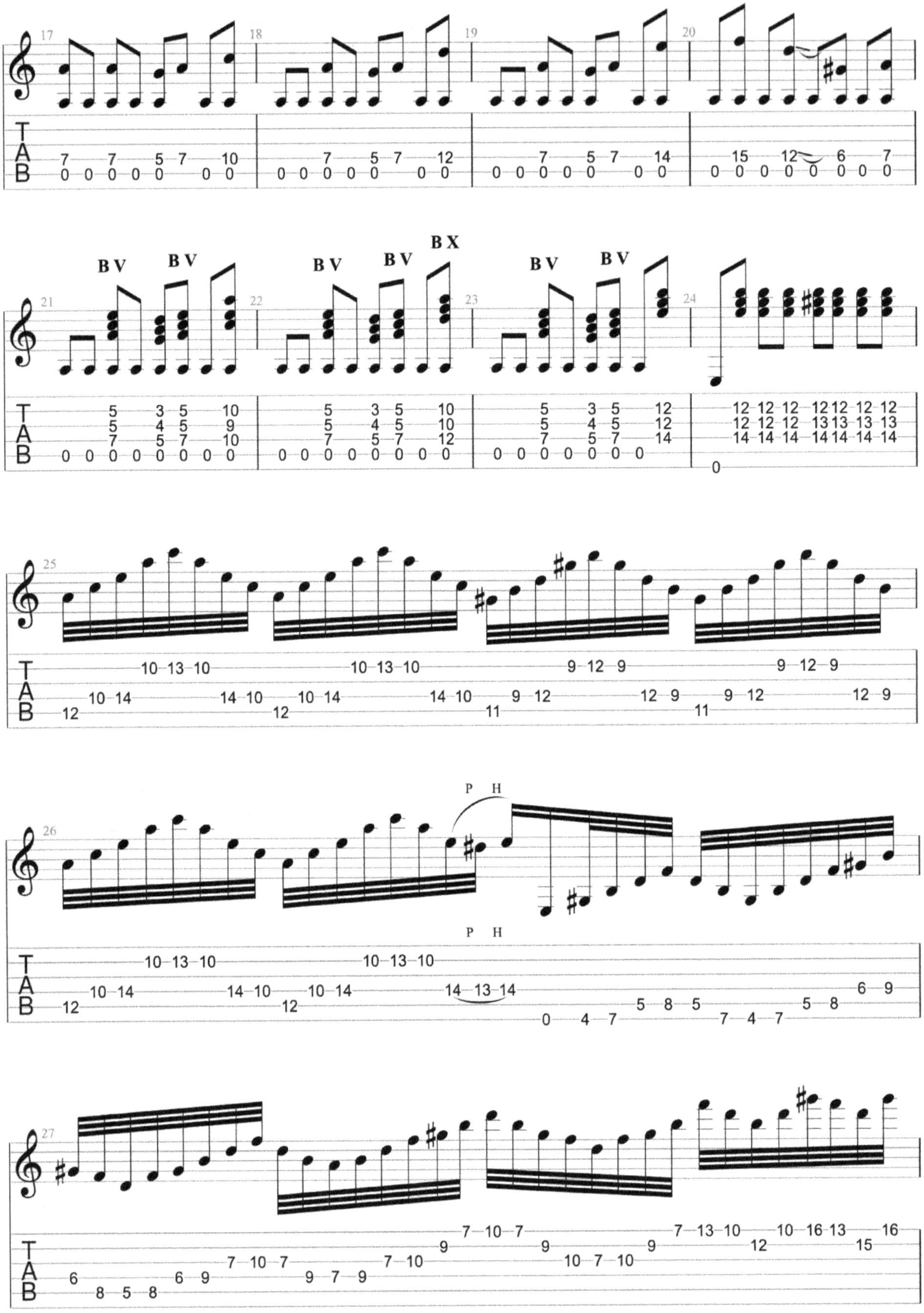
B V
B X
P H
TAB

As you find your musical voice and identity as a guitarist, it's important to ask yourself some guiding questions. Answering these questions for yourself will help shape your phrasing into mature statements, and may change the way you approach the fretboard or contribute to the music as a whole:

-What is the overall tone or emotion of the song, and how can my guitar expression add to it?

-how long are my phrases? In other words, how much space to I have to develop my ideas?

-Do I want to increase, decrease, or keep the same intensity?

-Am I leaving enough space to breathe between ideas?

-Am I targeting effective notes?

-What rhythmic or melodic sequences can I expand on?

-Is anyone else in the band playing a rhythmic or melodic idea I can respond to or play off of?

-What ornaments are appropriate for the song's style, and where should I put them to give my playing a strong identity?

-Do I want to melodically ascend, descend, or remain stagnant?

-Am I overdoing it? Does the expression call for a "less is more" approach?

-Was my expression effective or memorable?

-What would I change for next time?

The toolbox is yours, get building!

GLOSSARY

Alternate Picking(pg.67)- An alternating pattern between down strokes and up strokes.

Arpeggio(pg.22)- The breaking of a chord to play its notes one at a time.

Bend(pg.72)- The displacement of a string to increase its tension and raise its pitch.

Blue Note(pg.33)- Flat 3 in relation a key's major root and flat 5 in relation to the minor.

Cadence(pg.90)- A musical punctuation mark that finalizes an idea.

Cadence(Perfect Authentic) (pg.90)- A cadence in which the final chord lands in root position with the tonic as the highest note in the chord.

Cadence(Imperfect Authentic) (pg.90)- A cadence in which the final chord is inverted and/or a note other than the tonic is the highest note in the chord.

Cadence(Half)(pg.91)- A functional resting point in a musical idea, generally resting on a dominant chord and suggesting there is more to come.

Cadence(Rhythmic)(pg.91)- A resolution of anticipation through modification of an expression's rhythm.

Cadence(Deceptive)(pg.91)- The misdirection of the listener's expectations through a resolution to the six chord.

CAGED System(pg.30)- A specific arrangement of five chord shapes where each shape connects to the next, forming a connective network across the fretboard.

CAGED System (Pentatonic) (pg.32)- A specific arrangement of the five pentatonic forms (boxes) where each form connects to the next, forming a connective network across the fretboard.

CAGED System (Diatonic) (pg.34)- A Specific arrangement of the five diatonic forms (boxes) where each form connects to the next, forming a connective network across the fretboard.

Chord(s) (pg.11)- Three or more notes played simultaneously, measured by the intervals between notes.

Chord Additions (pg.16)- A basic triad (root, third, fifth) with the addition of the specified "add" note (usually 4,6,9, or 11).

Chord Extensions (pg.17)- A basic triad (root, third, fifth) with all thirds up to the specified extension (7,9,11, up to 13).

Chord Function (pg.93)- The tonal hierarchy of a key's diatonic chords and their relationship to the tonic.

Chord Suspensions (pg.17)- Chords that suspend (omit) the third and replace it with the second (sus2) or fourth (sus4) before resolving back to the third.

Chord Voicing (pg.15)- The construction of a chord with a specific ratio of roots, thirds, and fifths in a given fretboard region.

Chromatic Scale (pg.8)- A scale containing all twelve chromatic pitches.

Common Tone (pg.61)- A shared note between neighboring chords.

Compound Interval (pg.4)- Intervals that go beyond the octave (9ths through 14ths).

Crescendo (pg.89)- A gradual volume increase, notated by an expanding hairpin.

Cross Picking (pg.68)- Alternate picking a specific group of notes to arpeggiate a given chord.

Decrescendo (pg.89)- A gradual volume decrease, notated by a contracting hairpin.

Downpicking (pg.66)- The execution of a given passage of notes with down strokes only.

Drone (pg.60)- A reoccurring or sustained note that is generally assigned to a bass voice.

Economy Picking(pg.68)- The execution of a passage where each note is plucked in the direction of the next, defaulting to alternate picking when subsequent notes are on the same string.

Enharmonic(pg.12)- Notes that sound the same, but are written differently, such as E# and F.

Fingerstyle(pg.70)- The use of the thumb (p), index (i), middle (m), and ring (a) fingers to pluck the strings for a warmer tone.

Grace Note(pg.74)- A pre-emptive starting note with no rhythmic value.

Guide Finger(pg.83)- The use of a given finger to provide stability by staying on the same string when shifting between chords.

Half-Step(pg.4)- The distance between two adjacent notes, like C to C# on a keyboard or fret one to fret two on any string of a guitar.

Hammer-on(pg.63)- The use of a playing-hand finger to swiftly press a string into a given fret, sounding a note without plucking it with the strumming hand.

Harmonic(pg.78)- A higher frequency pitch in relation to a lower fundamental tone.

Harmonic(Natural)(pg.79)- Fractional relationships that present themselves across the open strings.

Harmonic(Artificial)(pg.79)- The preservation of a natural harmonic's fractional relationship, moved to a specific fret in order to sound an otherwise unreachable chromatic pitch.

Harmonic(Pinch)(pg.80)- The exposure of the strumming hand's thumb to make contact on the string while plucking to achieve a sharp squeal, generally used with high gain.

Harmonic Minor Scale(pg.9)- Similar to the natural minor scale, with the exception of the raised seventh scale degree:
Scale Degrees: 1 2 b3 4 5 b6 7

Harmonize (pg.26)- To play two notes in a given scale that are a specified distance apart, such as thirds or sixths.

Hungarian Minor Scale (pg.10)- Similar to the harmonic minor scale with the exception of the raised fourth scale degree:
Scale Degrees: 1 2 b3 #4 5 b6 7

Hybrid Picking (pg.70)- To maintain the use of a pick between the thumb and index finger, while incorporating the middle and ring fingers to pluck additional notes.

Interval (pg.4)- The distance between two pitches, usually measured in half steps.

Inversion (pg.19)- A re-arrangement of the notes in a given chord so that a note other than the root is on the bottom.

Inversion (first) (pg.19)- A chord re-arranged with a third in the bass.

Inversion (second) (pg.19)- A chord re-arranged with a fifth in the bass.

Inversion (third) (pg.19)- A chord re-arranged with a seventh in the bass.

Legato (pg.62)- Translated from Italian as "tied-together", played on a guitar by sounding a series of notes without directly plucking them.

Major Scale (pg.9)- The foundation of Western music, generally characterized as "happy" and "bright":
Scale Degrees: 1 2 3 4 5 6 7

Major Pentatonic Scale (pg.9)- A collection of five notes with the following scale degrees pulled from the Major Scale:
Scale Degrees: 1 2 3 5 6

Minor Pentatonic Scale (pg.10)- The counter-balance to the Major Pentatonic Scale, with the following scale degrees pulled from the Natural Minor Scale:
Scale Degrees: 1 b3 4 5 b7

Mode(pg.39)- A re-organization of the notes in a specified scale so that a different scale degree is prioritized as the starting note (tonic).

Motive(pg.97)- A small theme or group of notes that is legitimized through repetition.

Natural Minor Scale(pg.9)- The counter-balance to the Major Scale, indicating "sadness" or "darkness":
Scale Degrees: 1 2 ♭3 4 5 ♭6 ♭7

Neapolitan Minor Scale (pg.10)- Similar to the Harmonic Minor Scale, with the exception of the lowered second scale degree:
Scale Degrees: 1 ♭2 ♭3 4 5 ♭6 7

Octave(pg.2)- A collection of all twelve chromatic pitches, or an intervallic leap of twelve half-steps.

Palm-Mute(pg.77)- The use of the edge of the right hand's palm to roll past its resting point on the bridge to make contact with the strings.

Parent Key(pg.45)- The foundational key that a given mode derives its collection of notes from.

Passing Tone(pg.33)- A note played between two stable tones, usually suggesting chromaticism or color.

Phrasing(pg.96)- The way a musician shapes the notes of a passage to create a unique expression.

Position(s)(pg.3)- A four fret section of the fretboard, with one fret for each playing-hand finger.

Pre-Bend(pg.73)- To pre-emptively bend a string to pitch, then pluck the note and release the string down to its regular tension.

Pull-off(pg.63)- The use of a left hand finger currently ringing a given note to "pluck" the string, sounding a lower note on that same string (possibly the open string itself).

Rake(pg.77)- To scrape across several muted lower strings before digging into a note on a higher string.

Release(pg.90)- A resolution; the natural consequence of musical tension.

Root Position(pg19)- A chord arranged with a root in the bass.

Scale(pg.8)- A given collection of notes imparting a specific color on a musician's sound.

Scale Degree(s)(pg.8)- The classification of the notes within a given scale by their relative position to the starting note (tonic).

Seventh Chords(pg.12)- Chords with four notes stacked in thirds (root, third, fifth, and seventh).

Slide(pg.74)- The use of a left hand finger to transfer from one note to another on the same string.

Sweep Picking(pg.69)- To pluck multiple adjacent strings in a down-down-down or up-up-up picking pattern.

Target Note(pg.89)- Specific "identity" notes that imply a given chord or direction.

Tapping(pg.75)- The use of a right hand finger (or pick) to hammer-on and pull-off a note on the fretboard that would otherwise be unavailable to the left hand.

Tension(pg.87)- The anticipation a listener feels, creating a need for resolution.

Three Note Per String System (pg.37)- A connected network of forms across the fretboard, where each form has three notes from the diatonic scale on each string.

Tremolo Picking(pg.67)- The execution of a passage's notes via rapid alternating down and up strokes.

Trill(pg.76)- A rapid alternation between two notes, usually a half step apart.

Vibrato(pg.76)- To gently pull a note in and out of tune.

Warm Up(pg.52)- A session to refamiliarize oneself with the mechanics of their instrument.

Whole Tone Scale(pg.10)- A unique feeling of "floating":
Scale Degrees: 1 2 3 ♯4 ♯5 ♯6

ACKNOWLEDGEMENTS

This book would not have been possible without family, friends, and like-minded musicians I have had the pleasure of collaborating with. Thank you for the support, patience, feedback, and direction through my developing years. My sincere gratitude and appreciation go to the following people:

My parents Bruce and Doreen Vanderzyde

Judy Stringer, one of the most generous people I have ever met.

My highly skilled and dedicated guitar pedagogists and instructors:

-Ian Barry (Houston, Texas)

-Fernand Vera, DMA (Plano, Texas)

-Olga Amelkina-Vera, DMA (Plano, Texas)

-David Asbury, DMA (Georgetown, Texas)

-Jason Hoogerhyde, DMA (Georgetown, Texas)

My fellow musicians, friends, and favorite proof-readers:

Chanel Vanderzyde, Carl Lennartson, Kevin Jurica, Evan McPherson, Jacob Smith, Malik Qayumov, Matt Polo, Marco Polo, and Lee Risner.

Most importantly thank *you* for taking the time and energy out of your life to read through my book. I genuinely hope I was able to help you on your journey to musical development.

All the best,

Thomas Vanderzyde

ABOUT THE AUTHOR

Thomas Vanderzyde (b. 1996) is a Canadian musician, educator, author, and entrepreneur. No stranger to a good melody, some of his first memories center around listening to the Bee Gees in his family home in Vancouver, BC. Due to a disturbing lack of ice hockey after moving to Houston, Texas, Thomas picked up the guitar at age twelve in hopes of finding a new passion. His teenage years would be spent living under a rock trying to memorize album after album of Metallica, Iron Maiden, Megadeth, and Judas Priest discographies. Unable to find a University of Thrash Metal anywhere close to home, Thomas adapted to the classical guitar, discovering the world of Carcassi, Villa-Lobos, Tarrega, Mertz, and the like. Classically trained and armed with two degrees in music, Thomas now explores his own projects with an emphasis on musical passion, mastery, and creativity.

Thomas Vanderzyde holds an Associate of Arts degree from Collin College and a Bachelor of Music from Southwestern University. He now resides in Central Texas, where he spends his time composing, performing, recording, teaching, and otherwise sharing his love for the guitar with his ever-talented friends and fellow musicians.

Visit thomasvanderzyde.com for the latest updates and materials.

FURTHER READING

The following list of books encouraged countless lightbulbs to go off for me, significantly impacting my understanding of the guitar and music as a whole. Any and all of them make fantastic additions to any developing guitarist's library.

Edwards, Bill: *Fretboard Logic* (Bill Edwards Publishing, 1989)

Govan, Guthrie: *Creative Guitar 1* (SMT, 2003)

Herstand, Ari: *How to Make It in the New Music Business* (Liveright, 2017)

Heussenstamm, John: *Guitar Workout* (Hal Leonard, 2010)

Iznaola, Ricardo: *On Practicing* (Mel Bay Publications, 2000)

Klein, Jim: *Welcome to the Jungle* (Hal Leonard, 2013)

Kolb, Tom: *Music Theory* (Hal Leonard, 2005)

Palmer, Matt: *The Virtuoso Guitarist* (MP Music Co, 2008)

Ross, Alex: *The Rest is Noise* (Farrar, Straus, and Giroux, 2007)

Tennant, Scott: *Pumping Nylon* (Alfred Music Publishing, 1995)

Vai, Steve: *Vaideology* (Hal Leonard, 2019)